Kindergartens, Schools and Playgrounds

Kindergartens, Schools and Playgrounds

LOFT

Editorial coordination:
Cristina Paredes Benítez

Editors:
Ana Cañizares, Julio Fajardo

Translation:
Jay Noden

Art director:
Mireia Casanovas Soley

Layout:
Oriol Serra, Anabel Naranjo

Editorial project:
2007 © LOFT Publications
Via Laietana, 32 4.°, of. 92
08003 Barcelona, Spain
Tel.: 0034 932 688 088
Fax: 0034 932 687 073
e-mail: loft@loftpublications.com
www.loftpublications.com

ISBN: 978-84-95832-85-6

Printed in China.

LOFT affirms that it posseses all the necessary rights for the publication of this material and has duly paid all royalties related to the authors' and photographers' rights. LOFT also affirms that it has violated no property rights and has respected common law, all authors' rights and other rights that could be relevant. Finally, LOFT affirms that this book contains no obscene nor slanderous material.

The total o partial reproduction of this book without the authorization of the publishers violates the two rights reserved; any use must be requested in advance.

If you would like to propose works to include in our upcoming books, please email us at loft@loftpublications.com.

In some cases it has been impossible to locate copyright owners of the images published in this book. Please contact the publisher if you are the copyright owner of any of the images published here.

6	Introduction	
10	Arteks	El Puiet
18	Rios Clementi Hale Studios	LAUSD Primary Centers
26	Venhoeven Architects	Brede College
36	Cottrell & Vermeulen Architecture	NDNA Regional Center
44	Studio E Architects	Astronomy Classroom
50	Div. A Arkitekter	Kastellet Primary and Secondary School
60	Fabio Della Torre, Claudia Bigi	Arcobaleno Kindergarten
68	Div. A Arkitekter	Ringstabekk Secondary Institute
78	Buschow Henley	Performing Arts Hall at Caldicott School
86	G+W	Primary School in La Corita
94	Wingardh Architects	Mimers Hus
102	Atelier Central	Kindergarten in Bicesse
108	Wingardh Architects	Secondary Institute in Aranäs
116	nbAA	Kindergarten in Cacém
126	Winkler Architektur	Musikchule Gratkorn
132	Taller Básico de Arquitectura	Nursery and Surgery in Gorraiz
142	Andreas Treusch	Natorpgasse Primary School
150	AMP Arquitectos	Rafael Arozarena Secondary Institute
160	Marcos Acayaba	College in São Paulo
166	Dietrich Untertrifaller	Kindergarten in Egg
176	Randić Turato	Primary School in Croatia
184	Shuhei Endo	Bubbletecture
192	Boora Architects	Secondary Institute of Clackamas
200	C+S Associati	Kindergarten in Pederobba
208	ADP Architects	Western House Primary School
216	Richard Rogers Partnership	Minami Yamashiro Primary School
224	Machnè Architekten	Kindergarten in Leisach
232	Gruzen Samton Architects	Primary School in Babylon
240	John Friedman-Alice Kimm Architects	Expansion of Aragon Avenue Elementary School
248	Hermann Kaufmann	Bundesgymnasium Bludenz

INTRODUCTION

The projects compiled in this volume share a single raison d'être: education. This fundamental premise determines each of their features, and reminds us how important the service is that these buildings provide society, and of the need to develop this service in the best possible way. The concept that education is the basis of all social progress is nothing new. There is no evolution as important in society as the education of the individuals that compose it.

This is why the architectural development of these educational centers is so crucial, in particularly regarding nurseries, kindergartens, and schools. This volume illustrates the adaptation of numerous architectural solutions to the different stages of education, in different parts of the world. From the youngest students to eighteen-year olds.

The projects included in this collection have been chosen for their successful attempts to offer an environment and infrastructure appropriate for learning. They are also designed to promote togetherness and the exchange of knowledge and interests. School, as well as being a center of learning, is where we learn to think, share and live with one another. This is why it is so important that projects for these centers have all the necessary resources and innovations as well as the most appropriate spaces at their disposal.

Furthermore, school is no longer merely a building with classrooms in it. Many of the centers shown in this book also serve as a meeting place for the local community. For example, outside of school hours people in the area may make use of their libraries, assembly rooms or sports facilities.

Another aspect that distinguishes these projects from their more traditional counterparts is their "intelligence". These buildings are all designed to respect the environment and their careful planning maximizes energy savings. Each project has worked towards optimizing conditions of natural light and ventilation.

This book is a display of some of the most recent work carried out by architects from all over the world, in an attempt to stimulate the learning process of students of different ages, while also guaranteeing aspects as important as comfort and safety.

Kindergartens, Schools and Playgrounds

The project of this complex attempts to integrate with the traditional elements present in the surroundings. The façades, rather than adding a contemporary flavor, reinterpret the typical constructions and materials of the Andorran architecture, such as wood, stone and the roof work.

EL PUIET

Arteks

Ordino, Andorra, 2004
Photos © Eugeni Pons

The architects behind this complex accepted the challenge of providing a mountain village of 1600 inhabitants with a complex that would include a nursery, an apartment block, parking for 116 cars and a venue for exhibitions and conferences. The challenge, above all, was for the building to fit with the winding roads of the village, and not to alter the morphology of its surroundings too much. The difficulty of consolidating these premises with a project of 100,000 ft² are clear. Another of the project's difficulties was installing modern architecture in the setting of a traditional mountain village, whose legislation requires pitched roofs and stone cladding on the façades.

The constructed nursery has a capacity for 180 children, while the exhibition site is still undergoing construction.

Its integration into the urban landscape was complicated due to the dimensions of the site (89 x 315 ft), which had to be entirely occupied, and because the alignment of the streets could not be modified.

The complex has been designed as an enormous plinth whose structure consists of traditional materials, primarily stone. The volume that houses this multi-purpose venue takes advantage of the changing level between the two adjacent streets to obtain a twenty-foot elevation. The nursery building and apartment block are located above the multi-purpose venue, with an access atrium between the two.

A combination of roofs and volumes attempts to soften the impact of the complex, and a variety of heights gives the impression of a more varied skyline. The range of materials used also contributes to this effect.

East elevation

West elevation

North elevation

South elevation

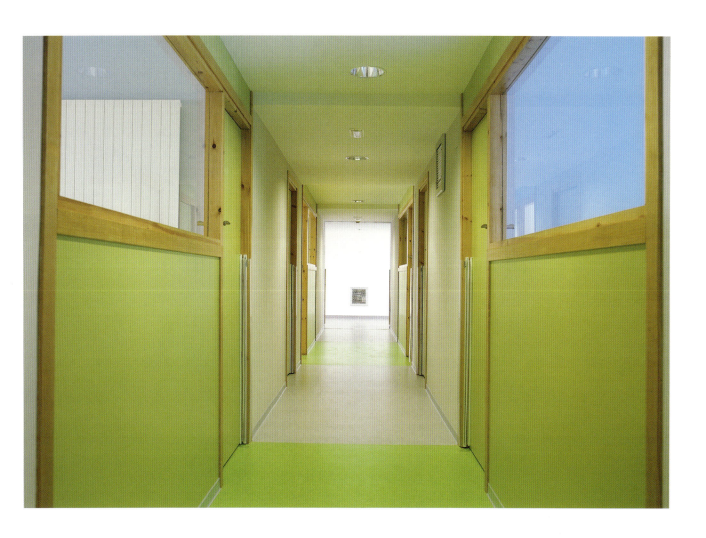

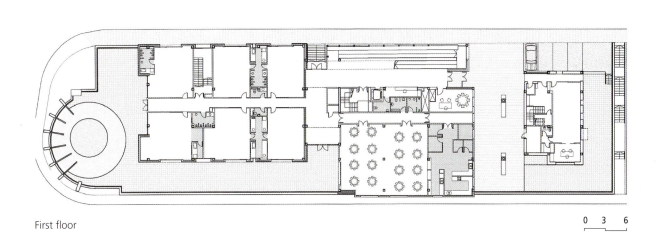

First floor

0 3 6

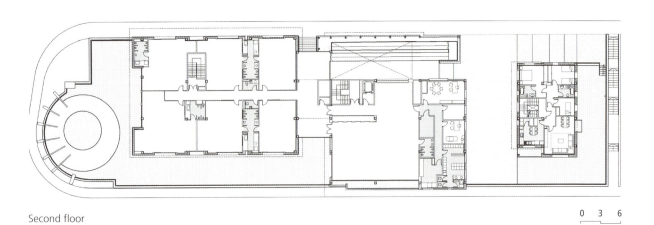

Second floor

The floor plans of the modules are identical, but each of their façades can be distinguished by a particular motif and different color schemes. Elements from nature decorate the preschool classrooms while those for the primary school are adorned with pictures of different forms of transport.

LAUSD PRIMARY CENTERS

Rios Clementi Hale Studios

Los Angeles, CA, United States, prototype
Photos © Tom Bonner

With the aim of reducing the size of the classrooms, the Los Angeles Unified School District created this school prototype for sites measuring between 1.5 and 3 square miles. The project allows reductions in both expenses and in the time invested in the construction.

The proposed modules each house a 23 x 26 foot "movable" classroom. These modules stand back-to-back allowing for windows in each of the three façades. An inverted roof has a space for high windows allowing the rooms to be flooded with natural light.

The entranceways for the dining area are built from steel and corrugated metal. The floors inside are covered, depending on the area, with gray carpet and gloss vinyl flooring. This part of the floor, like the furnishings for storage, changes color for each classroom to be able to distinguish one from another.

As with the modules for the classrooms, a prototype has also been designed for the site of the school. The exterior spaces have been designed to maximize their safety, with particular emphasis on flexibility. The different volumes, connected by walls, flank the perimeter of the complex. The sides of the site contain spaces that allow visual contact, from inside the school, with the surroundings. The courtyards serve as entranceways, can be used as "outdoor classrooms" and connect the modules of the different classrooms with a games area with running track and leisure facilities.

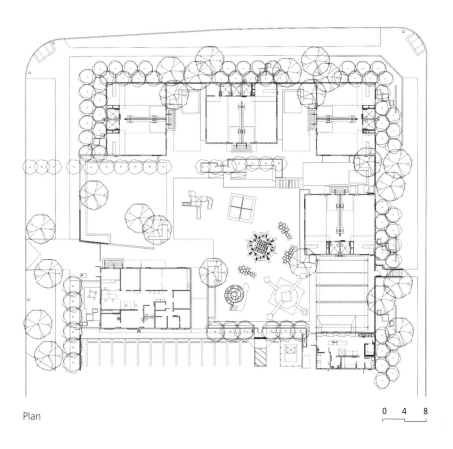

Plan

0 4 8

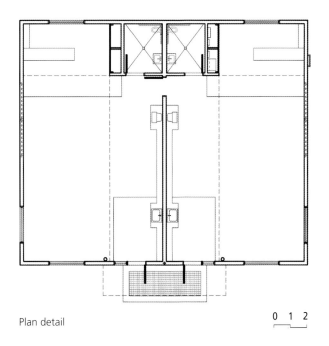

Plan detail

0 1 2

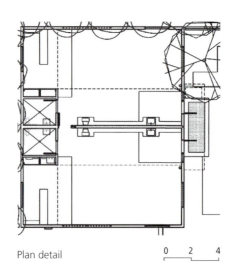

Plan detail 0 2 4

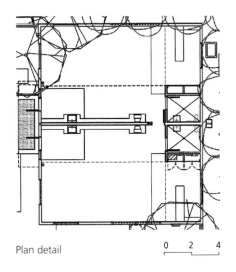

Plan detail

Most of the façade is covered in perforated aluminum panels. This metal parapet conceals, behind it, the electric installation and the various pipes. From top to bottom, these continuous panels leave spaces for windows of reinforced glass that open to the exterior of the building.

BREDE COLLEGE

Venhoeven Architects

Utrecht, The Netherlands, 2005
Photos © Luuk Kramer

A protected archaeological area, with Roman remains, is the setting for this complex, designed by Venhoeven Architects to house two primary schools, two day centers and a leisure center. The site, surrounded by orchards and green houses, still preserves elements from its agricultural past, such as the chimney, which constitutes a distinctive feature of the building.

From the beginning, it was designed as a compact building, which would benefit from the goodness of the surrounding nature. A basic idea was to offer versatile spaces that would adapt to different needs. With this premise in mind, it was decided, for example, to locate a games area on the roof.

Both the exterior and the interior of the building attempt to stimulate and connect with children's imaginations. The materials and structures used are sometimes more reminiscent of a space ship rather than a building, while its white base and dark gray roof also evoke the shape of a killer whale.

A covered, but perfectly lit, garden occupies the center of the floor plan, and serves as a games area for the children even when the weather is bad. This space also acts as a venue for meetings and as the entranceway to the school hall. The hall, suspended over this open area, backs on to the sports hall. When an event or celebration requires, the separation between the hall and sports hall can be eliminated to accommodate those in attendance.

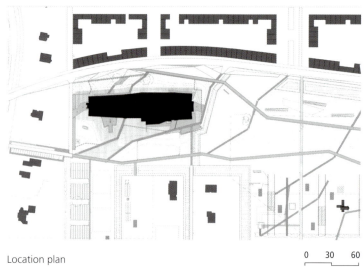

Location plan

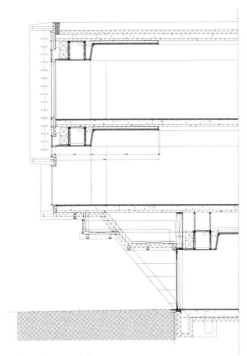
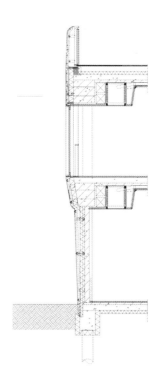

Construction details

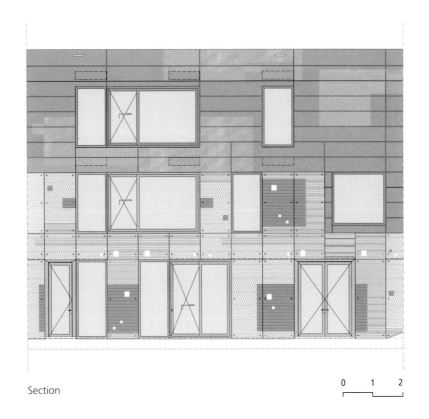

Section

0 1 2

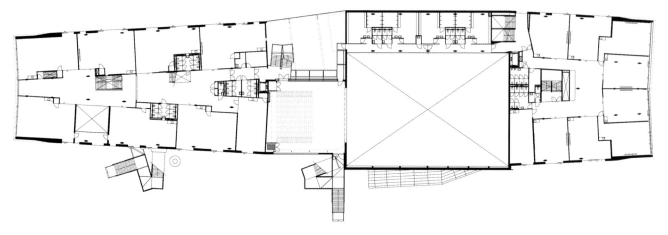

First floor

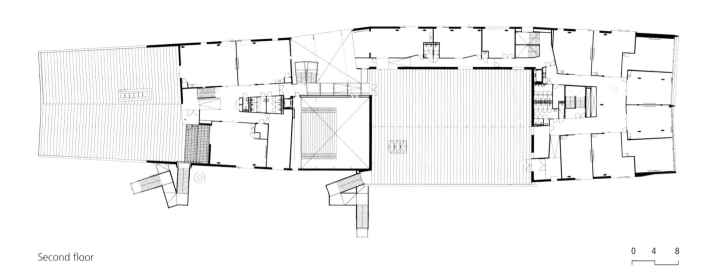

Second floor

0 4 8

The different spaces in the building have been designed as safe areas with zones for the different activities, maintaining the premise of offering a large children's space that is fun, and at the same time, easy to manage.

NDNA REGIONAL CENTER

Cottrell & Vermeulen Architecture

London, United Kingdom, 2004
Photos © Peter Grant

The NDNA (National Association of Day Nurseries) and Cottrell & Vermeulen organized workshops for parents and neighbors from the community to establish what the different needs of the project were, with the aim of creating a center that was personal, practical and attractive.

Initially this building was conceived as a huge translucent marquee with an aluminum parapet. Since British building regulations required a costly consolidation of this structure, a volume of glass reinforced plastic was chosen (Glass Reinforced Plastic, GRP) made in the United Kingdom.

The project is another step forward in Cottrell & Vermeulen's constant search for affordable architecture for children. Children occupy different spaces to adults and need outdoor areas for games. The interiors must also be fun for when the weather won't allow them to go outside. The overhanging roof on this building offers shelter to those who want to go outside on rainy days.

The site presented various problems concerning its environment. The close proximity of various main roads and Heathrow airport affected the air quality and caused a high level of noise. To improve the air quality, many trees and bushes were planted around the building, which has sound proofed roofs.

The building has various ways of saving energy, the most noteworthy being the condensing boiler, the photoelectric controls for the outdoor lighting and the drainage system of rainwater in the garden.

Location plan   0 5 10

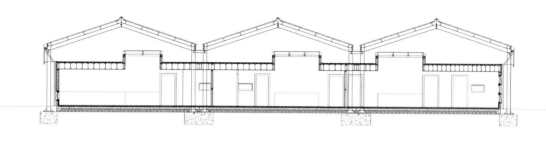
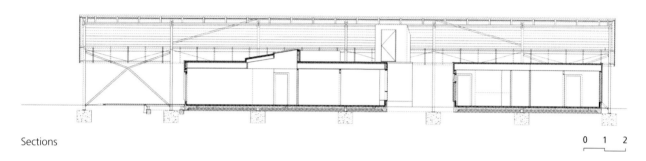

Sections

0 1 2

Construction detail

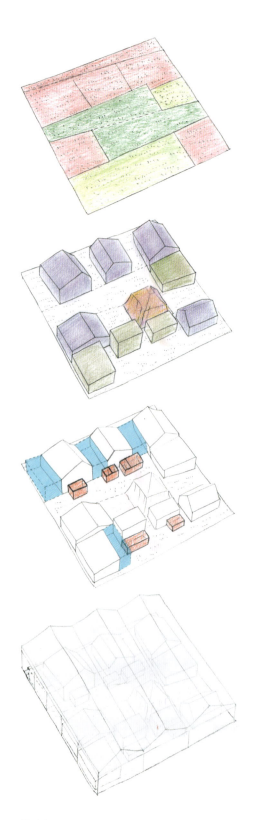

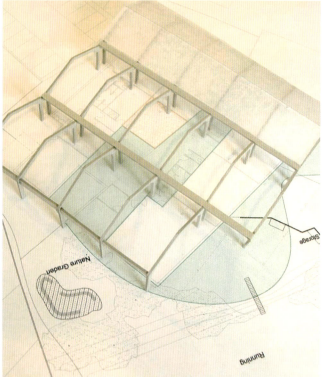

Sketches

Scale model

Most of the materials used in the construction of this "classroom of the future" are of natural origin, biodegradable, or come from recycled material, amongst which are some crossbeams from an old railway.

ASTRONOMY CLASSROOM

Studio E Architects

North Kensington, United Kingdom, 2003
Photos © Marie Louise Halpenny, Studio E Architects

Baptized "the classroom of the future", this project, financed by DfES (Department of Education and Skills) for the Royal Borough of Kensington and Chelsea, defies the conventional parameters of architecture in educational spaces. The main aim was to create an innovative and stimulating place of learning that would inspire pupils to develop their interests. This scientific classroom is an example of how subjects dealt with in classes can define the characteristics of the spaces they are taught in.

The resulting laboratory of astronomy includes a telescope, an indoor tropical garden and a wireless computer network.

The design work for the classroom began after numerous meetings between architects, teachers, pupils and members of the residents' association. The idea was that the opinions and suggestions from all these groups would be reflected in the final project. The building's role as a stimulating and thought provoking learning tool determined its geometry. It evokes the shapes of a human head, which opens to the outside via a greenhouse and explores the solar system by way of the telescope.

All the installations have been carried out to minimize both energy consumption and any environmental impact.

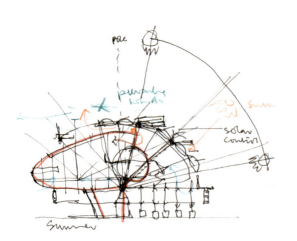

Sketch

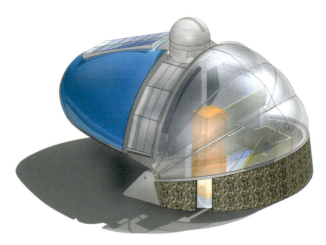

Render

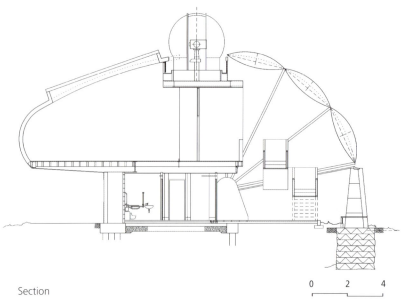

Section

0 2 4

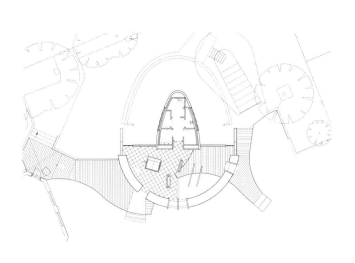

Ground floor

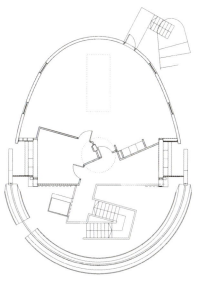

First floor

The staggered arrangement of courtyards and terraces underlines the projects aim of opening to the exterior. The exceptional natural surroundings allow the buildings to open to the courtyard through different levels of balconies.

KASTELLET PRIMARY AND SECONDARY SCHOOL

Div. A Arkitekter

Oslo, Norway, 2004
Photos © Div. A Arkitekter, Jiri Havran

This project, awarded in 2006 with an international RIBA prize for architecture, consists of a set of four buildings projected towards the exterior via terraces and balconies. The school, with a capacity of 560 pupils, is divided into departments for primary, middle and secondary school, with a special unit for children with disabilities. The location is a privileged one, the site's 75,000 ft² borders a forested area that belongs to the plot, allowing the architects to position the school facing this area, thus integrating nature with the daily lives of the pupils. In keeping with this idea, wood is the primary material used on the outsides of the buildings, which provide shade from the sun, and on the parquet roof of the courtyards that lead from the classrooms. Outside, the carefully designed landscape has an oriental feel to it, designed by Østengen & Bergo.

The hierarchy inside is in keeping with the curricular needs and the latest research into education, which receives recognition in Norway. These spaces have been given extraordinary flexibility, in such a way that classes can be conducted both in large rooms and in small tutor groups.

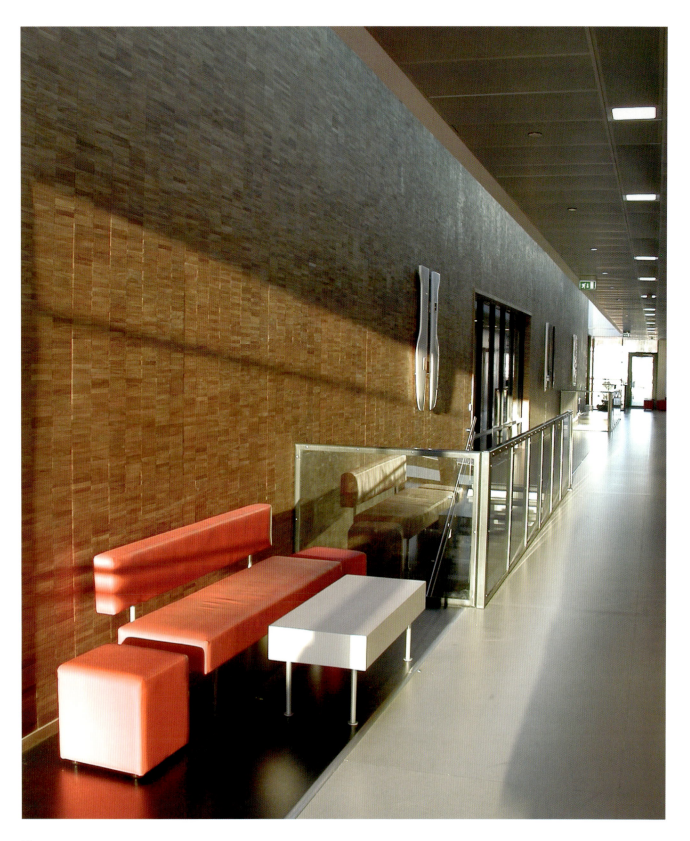

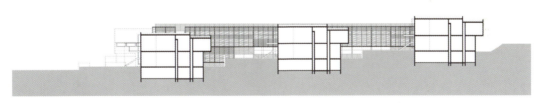

Section

0 5 10

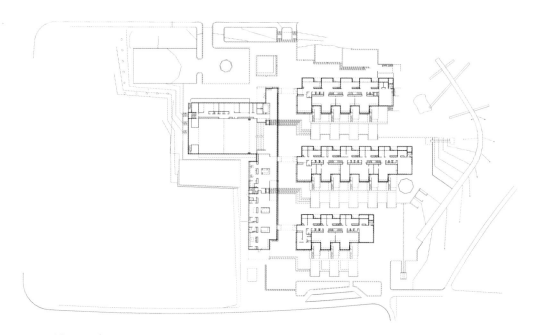

Ground floor

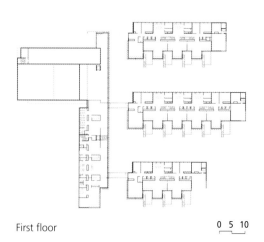

First floor   0 5 10

The two new volumes integrate with the exterior space by way of simple materials, such as the laminated roof and the painted ochre finishes on the façades. The result fits perfectly with the pre-existing constructions.

ARCOBALENO KINDERGARTEN

Fabio Della Torre, Claudia Bigi

Morbegno, Italy, 2005
Photos © Andrea Martiradonna

The extension project of this school included the construction of seven new classrooms. The kindergarten, occupies the same site as a nursery and a primary school, and belongs to a school campus, which is in turn integrated with the urban framework of the north of Morbegno, in the Italian province of Sondrio. Two new pavilions were constructed, located to the east and south of the main building, which house seven classrooms, with their own toilets and cloakrooms. The arrangement of these nine volumes, with respect to the existing school, allows each classroom to have easy access to, and a clear relation with, the main building.

The inclusion of smaller bodies next to the central structure allows each classroom to have a courtyard for toilets, as well as helping to create high quality learning spaces, based on an effective relation between the interior and the exterior. The arrangement of the classrooms has guaranteed a flow of abundant natural light.

Each classroom is a box whose longest sides act as dividing walls, covered by prefabricated wooden panels. The floor is laid in lino with an incorporated heating system.

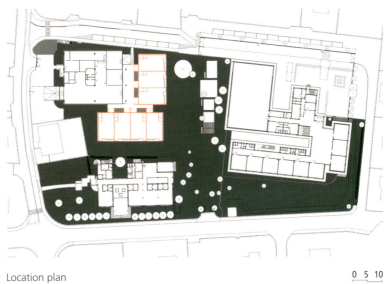

Location plan   0 5 10

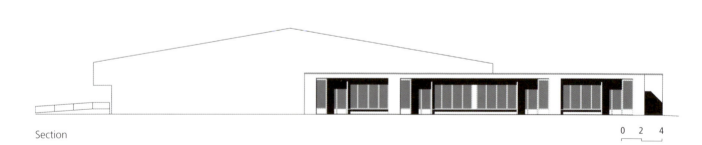

Section

0 2 4

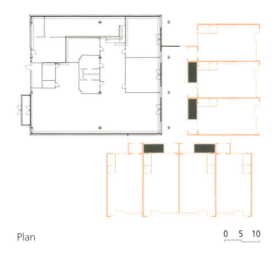

Plan   0 5 10

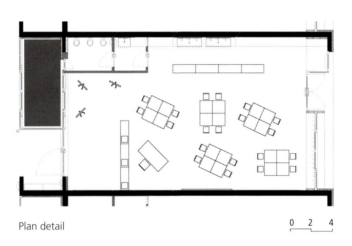

Plan detail   0 2 4

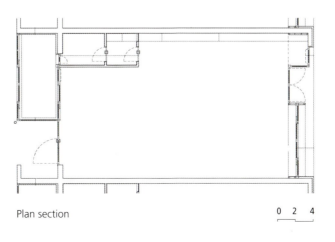

Plan section   0 2 4

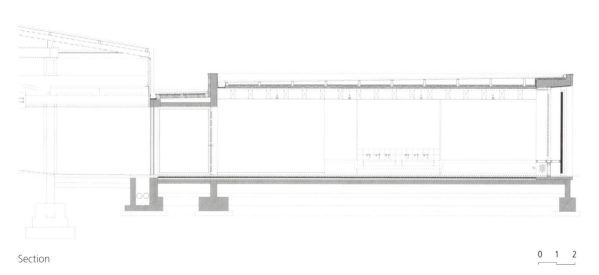

Section 0 1 2

The sources of natural light, at both ends, offer the classrooms ample light.

The building is clad in panels of untreated birch wood, as well as the pre-cast concrete and aluminum structure of the windows. The exterior spaces are designed to stimulate learning through the surroundings and the landscape.

RINGSTABEKK SECONDARY INSTITUTE

Div. A Arkitekter

Baerum, Norway, 2006
Photos © Div. A Arkitekter, Hugo & Åshild

For a long line of technical and economical reasons, when the Ringstabekk Secondary Institute, built in 1972, became out-of-date, it was impossible to carry out either a renovation or an extension. A new building had to be designed, whose project was handed to Div. A Arkitekter. The commission was to design a flexible building that could easily accommodate the different tendencies and pedagogical programs of the future. It was also important to make the most of the space, given the site's limited dimensions.

The design dossier presented underlined the need to consider the relationship between new pedagogical methods and modern architecture. The architects proposed a space that would stimulate the pupils' creativity and awaken their interest to learn. The resulting arrangement can accommodate very different teaching methods, both theoretical and practical.

The spaces of the resulting building vary both in size and nature, and range from small classrooms for tutorials to large auditorium style halls for sixty students. The communal central space can accommodate the entire student community. The complex has a mechanical ventilation and underfloor heating system.

Location plan 0 15 30

East elevation

West elevation

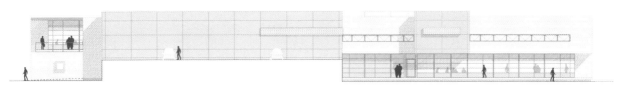

North elevation

South elevation

0 2 4

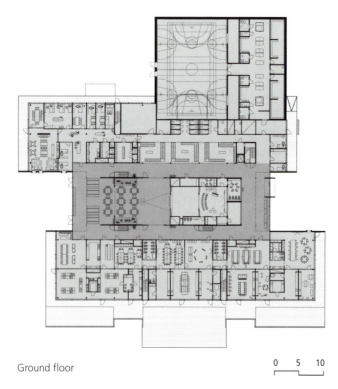

Ground floor

0 5 10

First floor

0 5 10

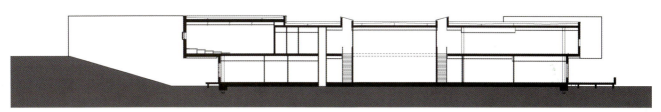

Section

0 2 4

The atrium that precedes the volume of the auditorium rises as an independent tower. A wooden pergola that extends the full width of the structure, providing the volume's interior with shade, has softened the façade. In the future, this can be used to support climbing plants.

PERFORMING ARTS HALL AT CALDICOTT SCHOOL

Buschow Henley

Farnham Royal, United Kingdom, 2004
Photos © Nick Kane

In 2002, Buschow Henley's studio won the project competition for the performing arts hall that Caldicott College wanted to build to commemorate its centenary. The building has replaced the previous hall that had fallen into disuse, and offers a cultural space to students, parents and community groups. As well as the main performance area, the volume houses three classrooms, a meetings room for teachers on the upper level, a second multi-purpose room and toilets. One premise for the college was for the new building not to affect the ventilation, light and size of the existing adjacent installations. It was also important that it integrated with the rest of the college to form part of a whole and that it was open to its surroundings and not a closed space. To comply with these premises, the new auditorium building was built about half a floor below the level of the grounds. This avoided casting shadows over nearby buildings and reduced the volume's impact on the landscape.

The materials used were chosen for their links with traditional architecture, and bring the project closer to the other installations in the college. All walls that lead from north to south are red brick, in keeping with the Victorian façade of the main building. The entrance tower and roof are surfaced in copper.

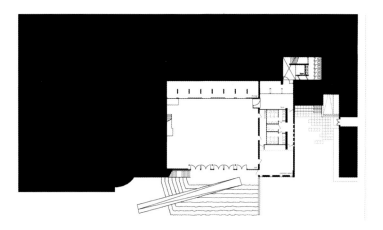

Ground floor

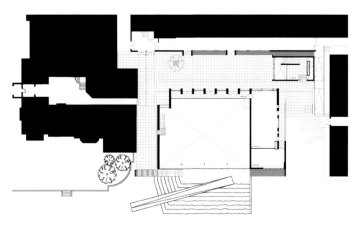

First floor

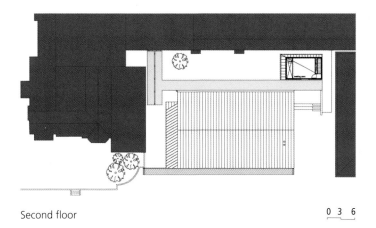

Second floor

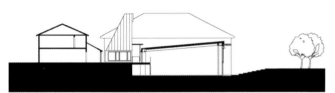
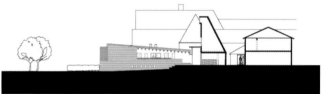
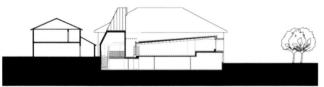
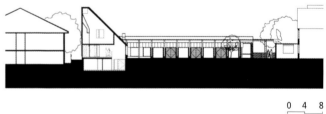

Sections

0 4 8

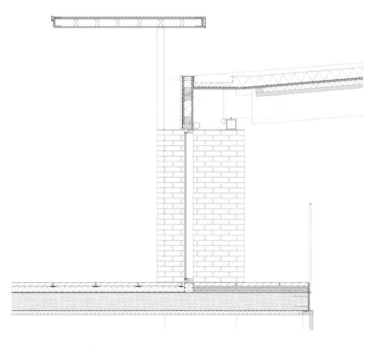

Construction detail

The magnificent presence of the pavilion owes a lot to its transparent façade, which overlooks the clearing and lights it up at night.

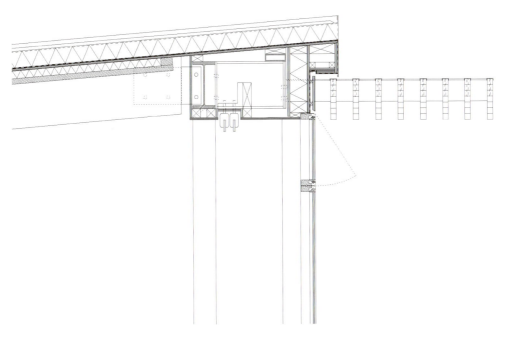

Construction detail

The façade that opens onto the central courtyard has one of the project's most striking features, the cellular polycarbonate panels in varying shades of blue. The north, east and west sides are surfaced in Trespa panels.

PRIMARY SCHOOL IN LA CORITA

G+W

Valdemoro, Madrid, 2005
Photos © Miguel de Guzmán

La Corita, a mainly residential area of Valdemoro, on the outskirts of Madrid, plays host to this primary school and playgroup. The two-story building looks onto a large south-facing courtyard and backs onto a residential estate. The west wing houses the playgroup, and the school is located in the central section, while the toilets of both centers are on the east side of the complex. The teachers' area —with cloakrooms, rest room and resources area— are located on the first floor.

The volume rises around a central courtyard, to which it is joined by an eminently translucent façade, which is fragmented by different openings.

The roofs of the building have various pools of colored light that illuminate the classrooms differently depending on the time of day and the season. This helps the little ones to develop their notion of things as being temporary.

The division of the courtyard is in keeping with the different activities that take place there. There are areas with rubber flooring, others with flattened earth, gardened areas and a vegetable patch. The importance of these different types of surfaces comes from the fact that the children spend a lot of their time sat or rolling around on them. The project, therefore, attempts to give them a better understanding about their learning place, by delineating the different areas with floors of different textures and colors.

Render

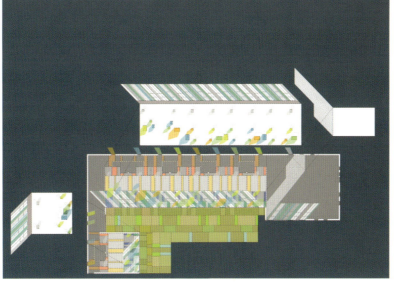

Lights and entrances

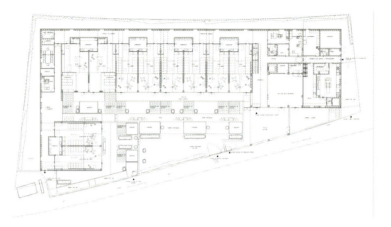

Ground floor

First floor

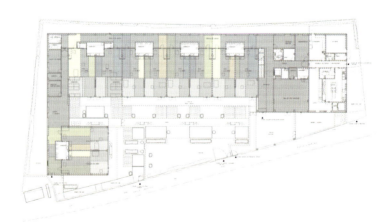

Floors

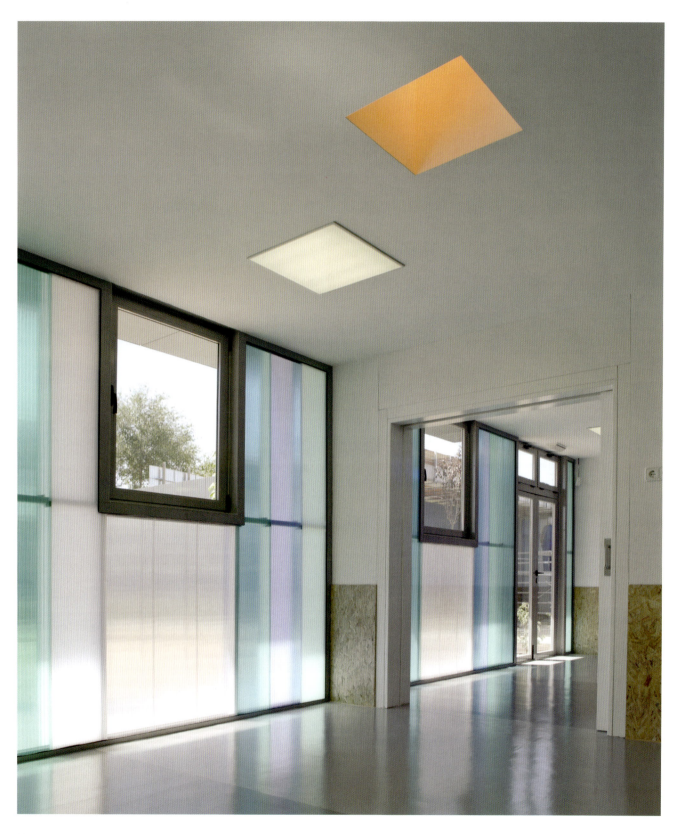

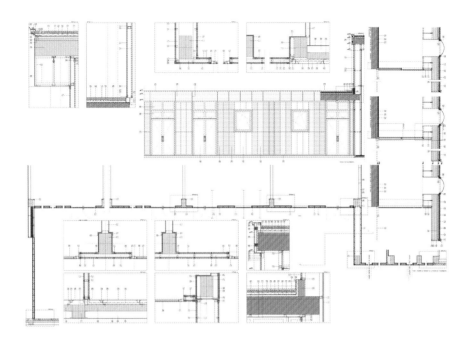
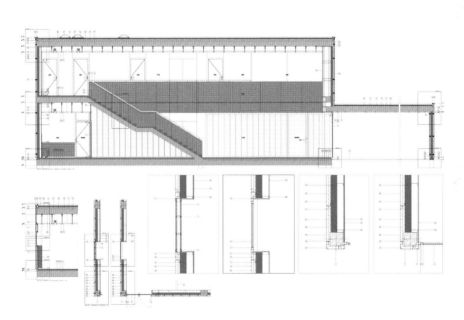

Construction details

A framework of vertical and horizontal concrete laminates acts as a filter to the sun and lends character to the building's exterior, with its grid of white strips. The light filters in through glass panels between the laminates.

MIMERS HUS

Wingardh Architects

Kungälv, Sweden, 2004
Photos © Ulf Celander

This complex, located in a corner of Kungälv's town center, to the north of Gothenburg, houses a secondary institute, as well as an auditorium and a library for students and the rest of the community. The low budget project required a simple design with façades of prefabricated elements. The use of laminates that cover the building's exterior, combined with the glass from the windows, follows the objective of keeping construction costs low. In contrast with these materials, the birch wood panels inside help to create a warm atmosphere. The inevitable austerity of the elements inside is compensated by the use of vivid colors to create cheerful spaces.

The architects' proposal divided the structure into four volumes. The first building, with the library, theater and arts room occupies the front section, facing the city. Another two buildings with classrooms are connected through a communal study area, while the fourth building is a sports hall that seats 300 people. To create a covered access passageway to the two existing buildings, which were integrated into the project, one of the streets had to be resurfaced.

Particular emphasis has been placed on facilitating access for people with disabilities, especially to the auditorium. The entrance is at the same level as the fourth row, which, in turn, is at the same height as the stage.

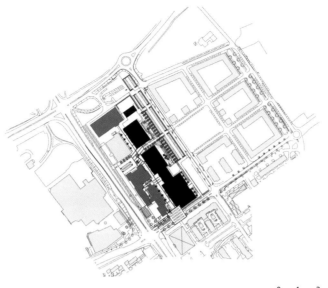

Location plan

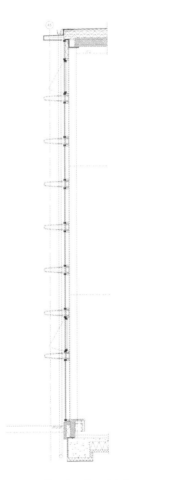

Construction detail

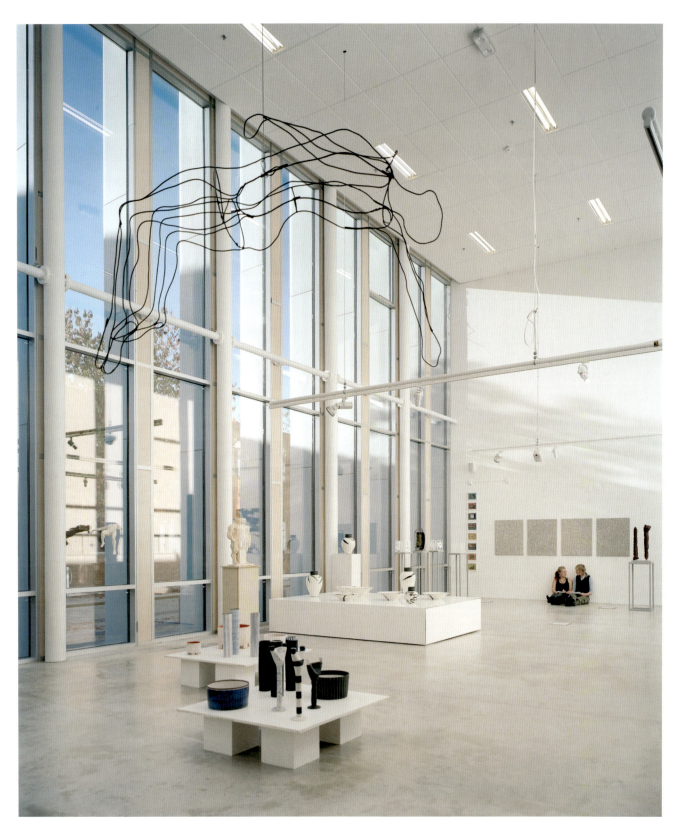

The gallery opens onto the study room in an open-plan and well-lit space.

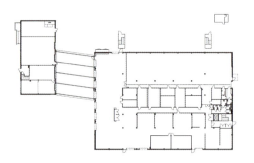
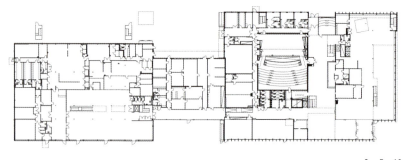

Second floor

0 5 10

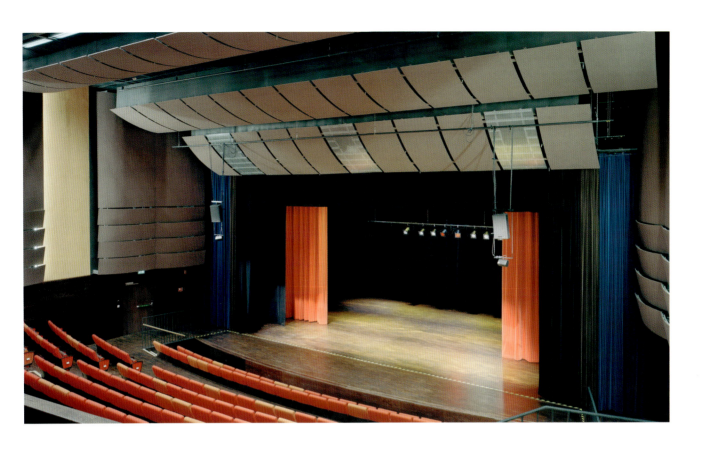

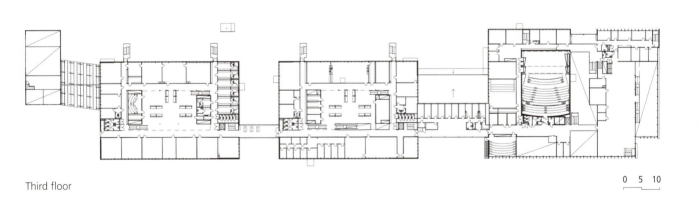

Third floor

0 5 10

The building has been designed with simple lines, and shapes that harmonize without clashing. The longitudinal axis of the passageway determines the shape of the volume and the distribution of the adjoining spaces, which corresponds to the different functions and academic years of the *kindergarten*.

KINDERGARTEN IN BICESSE

Atelier Central

Estoril, Portugal, 2005
Photos © Fernando Guerra, Sergio Guerra

For the project of this nursery school, the architects from the Atelier Central studio wanted to incorporate references from the world of children's imaginations. They also wanted to play with combinations of opaque and translucent surfaces. One distinctive aspect of the building are the circular skylights in the roof.

The shapes of the new construction are reminiscent of pieces from the children's game, Lego, arranged lengthways and aligned with the gallery. The passageway evokes and alludes to the students' evolution throughout the different years of kindergarten. It begins in the nursery, the most protected area, and ends in the area for the five-year olds, next to the entrance. As well as being the project's neurological center, the passageway also constitutes a barrier between the children's areas and the center's management and administration sections. Its translucent glass allows light to enter the different interiors during the day, and at night, here, light from inside can be seen outside.

A wall that surrounds the school separates two recreational areas: a small protected courtyard close to the refectory, with a fountain and cork tree, and another, bigger games area, next to the classrooms.

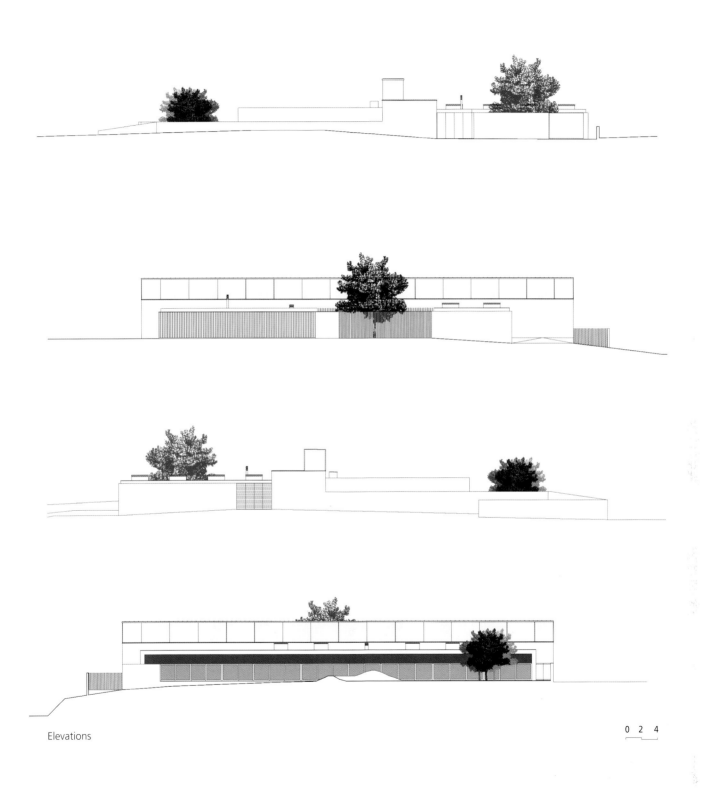

Elevations

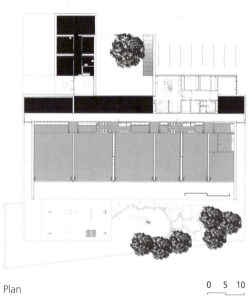

Plan

0 5 10

The façades, which use materials of pre-cast concrete, have, at their highest level, the projects most distinctive feature. On bases finished with different shades of ochre, the last section of the building's exterior displays large white symbols that refer to the different areas of learning and the subjects taught in the center.

SECONDARY INSTITUTE IN ARANÄS

Wingardh Architects

Kungsbacka, Sweden, 2006
Photos © Ulf Celander & Krister Engström

The extension of this secondary institute in the Swedish town of Kungsbacka divided its 1500 students into three groups of 500. Two newly constructed triangular structures housed two of these groups, while the third continued to occupy the large existing building, which was partly reconstructed. These groups of 500 were, in turn, split into groups of 100, and the communal and study spaces of each of the areas correspond to this division, designed to guarantee the comfort and appropriate integration of the institute's students. With the same aim in mind, the central courtyards act as entranceways to the classrooms and the school hall. Each group's area has a large communal space, with a neighboring teachers' area. The project avoids overcrowding by physically separating the different groups of pupils, although their allocation to one area or another does not stop them from making full use of all the installations.

The size and luminosity of the communal areas is quite striking. The dark parquet of the floor contrasts with the lightness that the numerous skylights afford, and with the use of colorful furnishings. The high ceilings and abundance of translucent surfaces help to make these spaces open and welcoming.

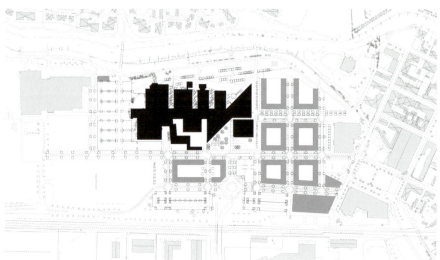

Location plan

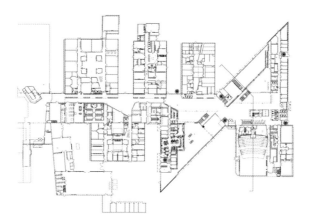

Ground floor

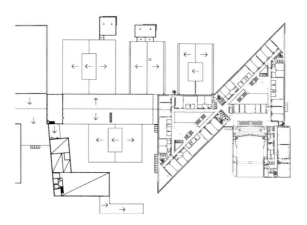

First floor

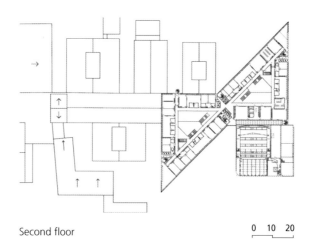

Second floor

0 10 20

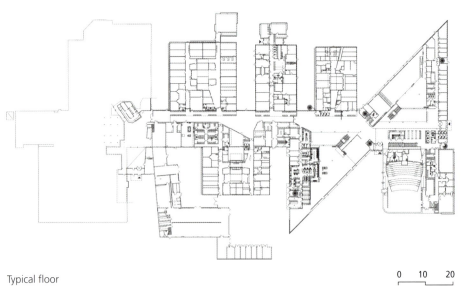

Typical floor

0 10 20

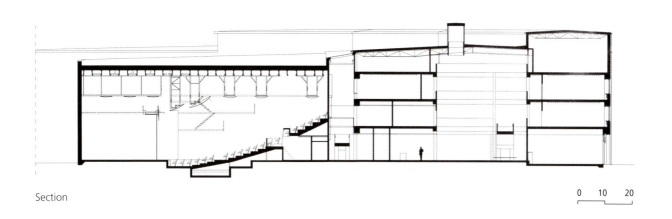

Section

0 10 20

The building is made from white reinforced concrete. The south façade is surfaced in panels of a darker aggregate-cement. On the inside, this structure is covered by thermal insulation and lined by a brick wall.

KINDERGARTEN IN CACÉM

nbAA

Cacém, Portugal, 2005
Photos © Fernando Guerra, Sergio Guerra

The aims of this nursery school project, among others, was to guarantee the center's easy access, and visually link it with the neighboring park and natural surroundings. It had to be south facing so as to favor the classroom areas, and also to allow these to open onto the green areas. It was also made clear from the start that the building would use passive energy systems, and that a central passageway would divide the work areas and guarantee clear spatial distinctions.

On the ground floor, an opaque and translucent volume, depending on the area, separates the entry and parking from the children's interior garden. This volume contains stairs and elevators to access the two upper floors, where a large hall connects to the central passageway. The classrooms are located on the south side, while the management and administration spaces occupy the north flank.

The first floor accommodates the kindergarten and includes the secretarial area, gymnasium and reading room. The classrooms have privileged positions with views over the garden. On the second floor are the toilets and study room. The heating system functions as a combination of solar panels and the boiler, which keeps the water hot and also provides heat to the underfloor heating installation. A rainwater collecting system directs water directly to a deposit, where it is then used for the toilet cisterns.

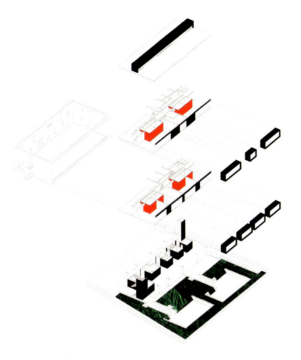

Axonometric view

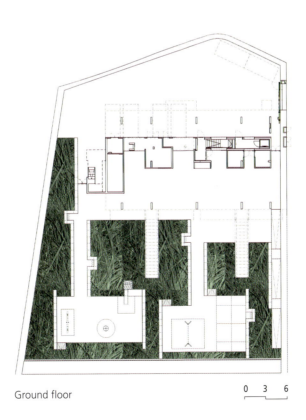

Ground floor

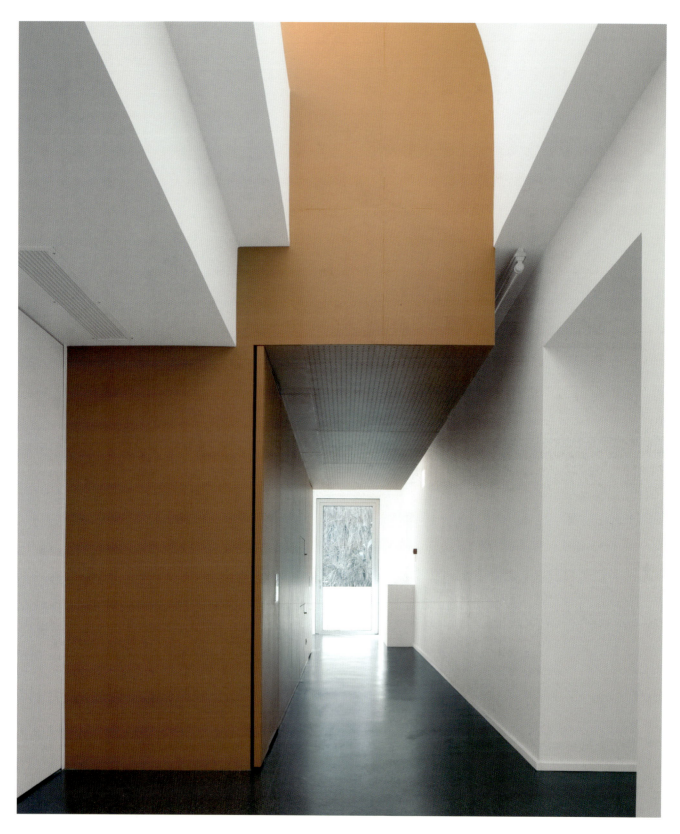

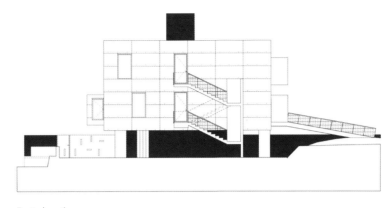

East elevation

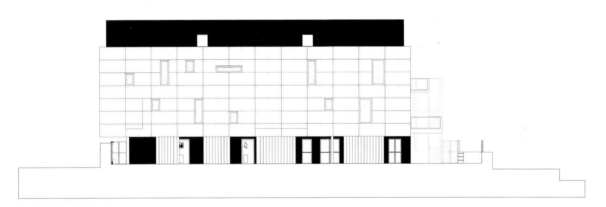

North elevation

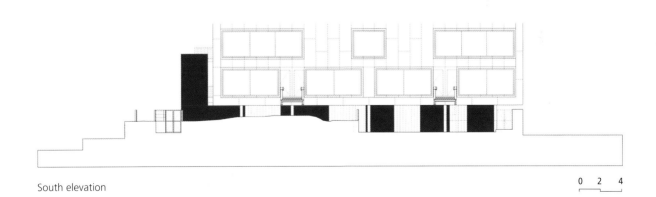

South elevation

0 2 4

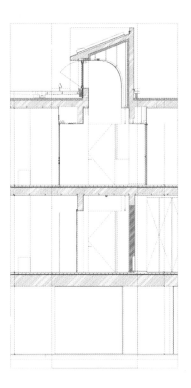
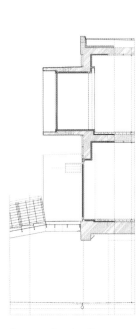
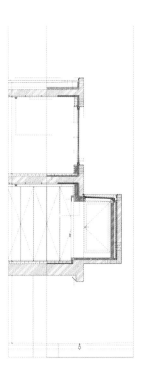

Construction details

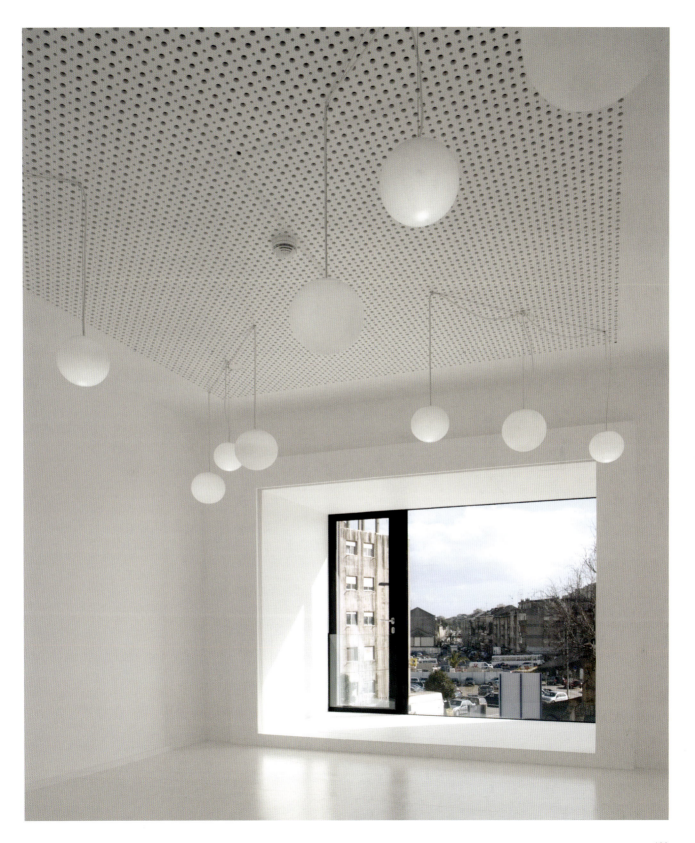

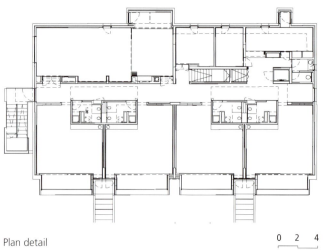

Plan detail

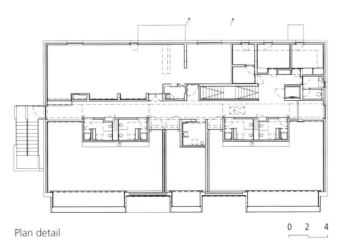

Plan detail

0 2 4

The communal areas and passageways are associated with glass, a constructive feature present in the opening between the two buildings and on the ground floor before the hall. The colored translucent panels create a cheerful atmosphere, which contrasts with the light gray walls.

MUSIKCHULE GRATKORN

Winkler Architektur

Styria, Austria, 2005
Photos © Paul Ott

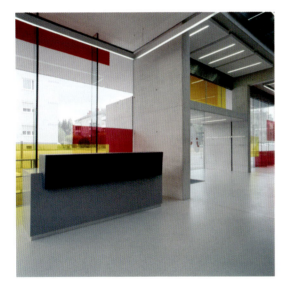

The existence of a small plot next to the Gratkorn secondary institute, which had not been built on, was the starting point for the construction of this music school. The initial analysis showed a series of synergies, one of which being that the new volume would be connected with the existing one on all three of its levels, so that both buildings could make use of the connecting hall on the ground floor. This also gave rise to classrooms and offices being created above it on the first and second floors. This layout allowed both buildings to share the same technicians, electricity and water supply etc…

The project proposed the transformation of cubic structures into more open spaces.

In areas where fewer people pass the walls are more solid, made from sandblasted concrete, and include thermal insulation. The interior has been soundproofed, which, being a music school, is of vital importance.

An indoor, glass greenhouse allows natural light to reach a lot of the rooms, and adds a touch of nature to the center of the building.

The multi-purpose volume, situated at street level, is a two-story space and extends to the north, housing the administrative area and reading and rehearsing rooms.

Ground floor

First floor

Second floor

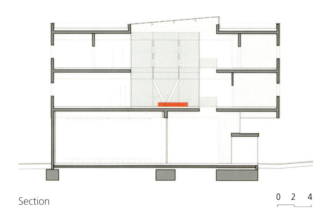

Section

The auditorium is a large and highly versatile space, which stands out for the acoustic insulation of its walls and ceilings.

The roofed area, both refreshing in the summer and protective in the winter, acts as a meeting place for parents of children in the nursery and patients from the surgery. The blocks have been designed more as a continuation of the covered space than as independent volumes.

NURSERY AND SURGERY IN GORRAIZ

Javier Pérez-Herreras and José V. Valdenebro García, Javier Quintana de Uña (collab.)/Taller Básico de Arquitectura

Navarra, Spain, 2004
Photos © Gogortza & Llorella

A principle of functional clarity marks the three volumes of this project: the nursery, the surgery and the covered square that acts as an access point to the two blocks.

The structure that covers the square is the joining feature of the project. Its luminosity and primary function of giving shelter in bad weather conditions link the project with its rural surroundings.

The respective organizational systems of the nursery and the surgery were carefully considered when designing the building, so the floor plan would not hinder but contribute to the smooth running of both centers.

The aerial plan provides the strongest image of the complex, which is also noteworthy for its transparent bubbles, irradiating light and offering views from outside of the building of the work taking place inside. This is especially the case at night.

The façades and volumes of the project display both its organization and its cross-section's mobility, underlining the idea of a horizontally composed architecture of bubbles.

Both the nursery and the surgery have been designed as a discrete continuation of their surroundings, intimately displaying the functionality of their interiors.

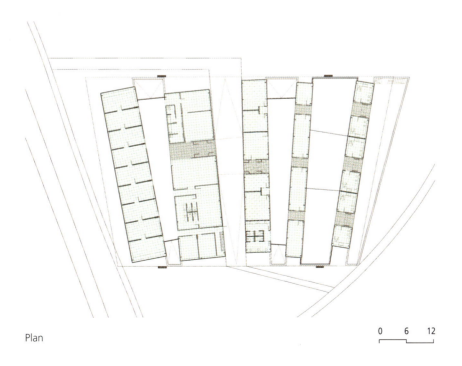

Plan

0 6 12

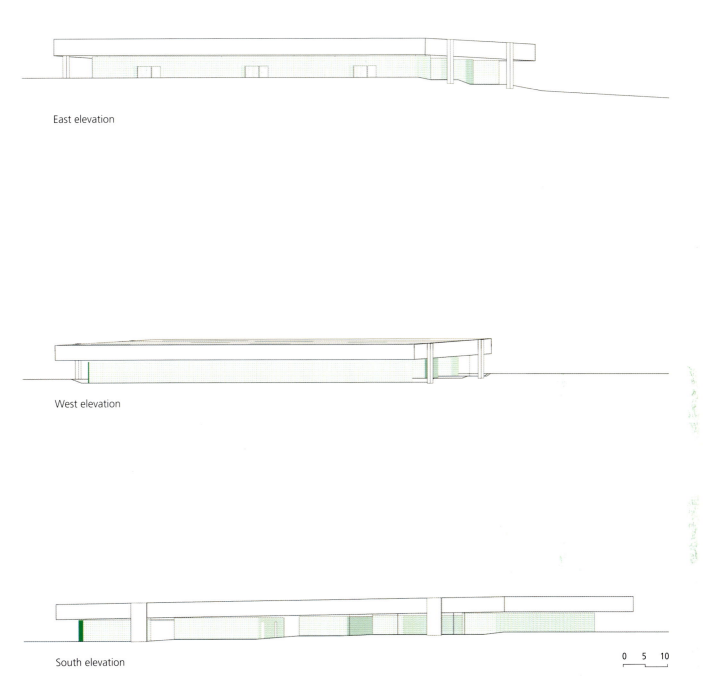

East elevation

West elevation

South elevation

0 5 10

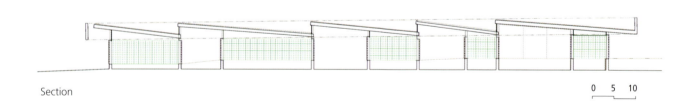
Section 0 5 10

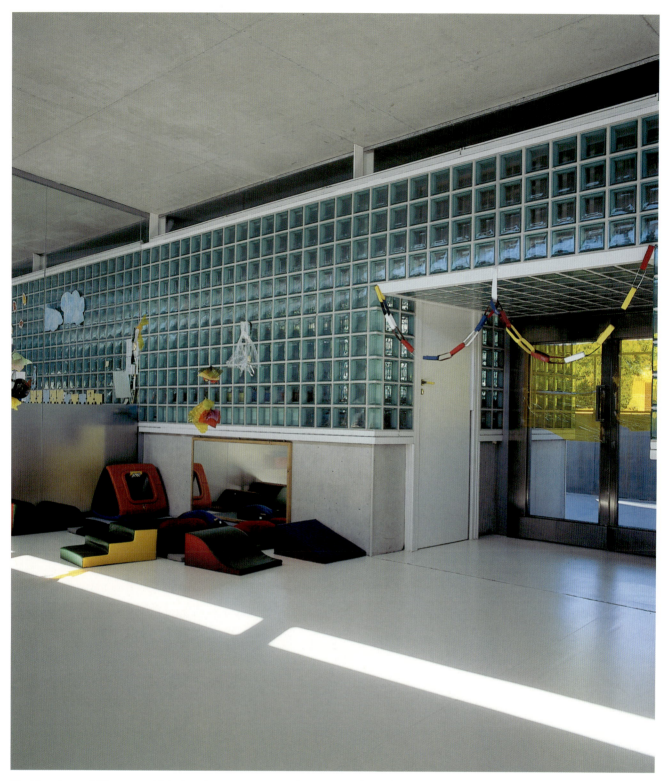
The blue glass wall filters natural light into the passageway, creating an atmosphere of warmth.

Given its monumental character, everything added was introduced in an attempt to combine the original artistic criteria with the latest technical innovations. Above all, the original structure was respected.

NATORPGASSE PRIMARY SCHOOL

Andreas Treusch

Vienna, Austria, 2001
Photos © Rupert Steiner

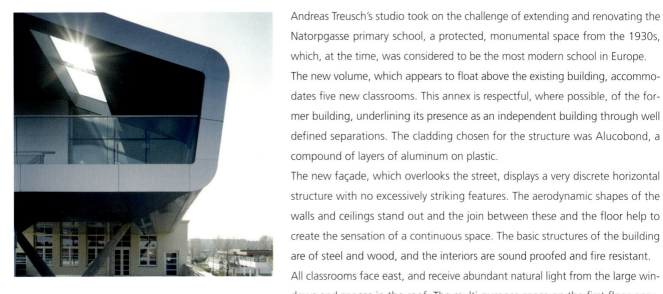

Andreas Treusch's studio took on the challenge of extending and renovating the Natorpgasse primary school, a protected, monumental space from the 1930s, which, at the time, was considered to be the most modern school in Europe.
The new volume, which appears to float above the existing building, accommodates five new classrooms. This annex is respectful, where possible, of the former building, underlining its presence as an independent building through well defined separations. The cladding chosen for the structure was Alucobond, a compound of layers of aluminum on plastic.
The new façade, which overlooks the street, displays a very discrete horizontal structure with no excessively striking features. The aerodynamic shapes of the walls and ceilings stand out and the join between these and the floor help to create the sensation of a continuous space. The basic structures of the building are of steel and wood, and the interiors are sound proofed and fire resistant.
All classrooms face east, and receive abundant natural light from the large windows and spaces in the roof. The multi-purpose space on the first floor occupies an area used by a classroom, which has been moved to the new structure, and now faces the upper courtyard.

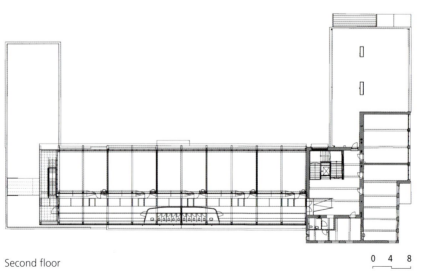

Second floor

0 4 8

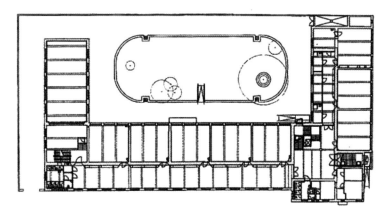

Ground floor

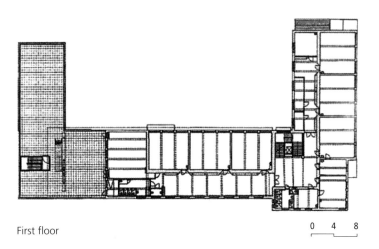

First floor

0 4 8

The elevator shaft is surrounded by a glass structure to allow light to pass and to guarantee a sensation of size on the stairs.

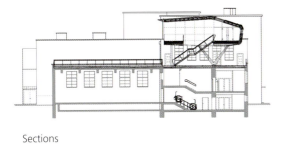

Sections

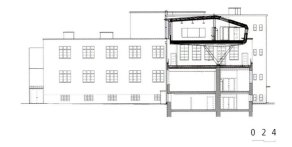

0 2 4

The building's concrete finish has been softened by light colors to link the building with the tones of the city's façades, and to relate it with the colors of the rural area to the southeast.

RAFAEL AROZARENA SECONDARY INSTITUTE

AMP Arquitectos

Tenerife, Spain, 2004
Photos © Miguel de Guzmán

A site very close to the historical center of the town of La Orotava, on the island of Tenerife, houses this center designed by AMP Arquitectos. The building integrates perfectly with the local topography, and rises as a distinctive feature on the surrounding urban landscape.

The block, which has been built under the premise of minimizing the costs of the work and its maintenance, occupies what was the site of a wide agricultural terrace, which stretched at some points past the stone walls.

To facilitate access, the main entrance is located on the southeastern slope and opens onto the only horizontal street that joins the site. The caretaker's office and administration offices are located on this level. The library is next to the entrance.

Most of the school activities take place on the two levels below that of the entrance, which contain numerous southeast-facing classrooms. A story below this are the science laboratories and computer rooms. The cafeteria is located below the main stairwell.

At the north end, much lower than the rest of the site, are the sports facilities, built below ground level to lessen their visual impact and to avoid blocking views that the building behind has of the valley and the sea.

Location plan

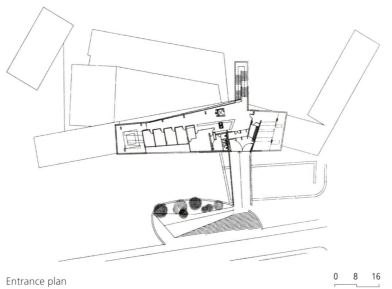

Entrance plan

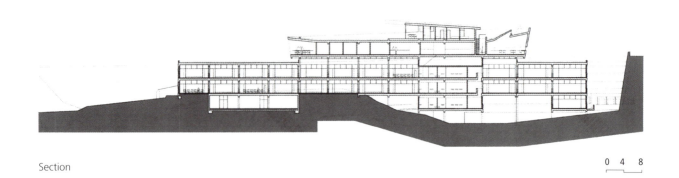

Section

0 4 8

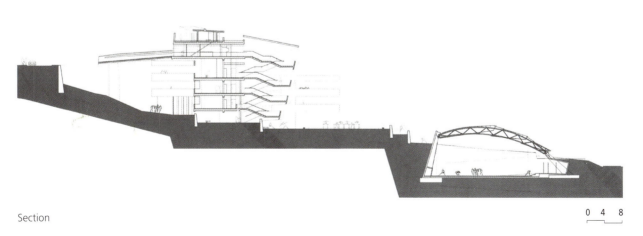

Section

0 4 8

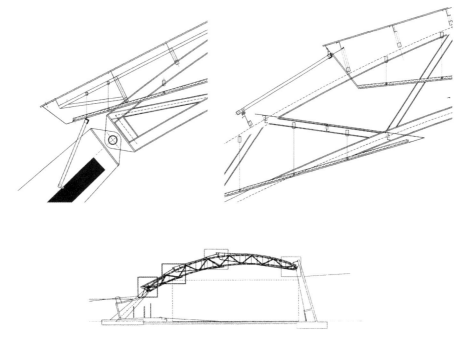

Construction detail of roof

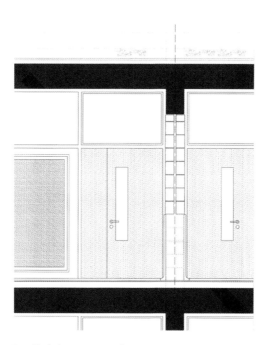

Detail of classroom envelope

This project's distinctive features are the pre-cast concrete structure of the different blocks and the metal roof installed over the covered courtyard. Four frames resting on the concrete pillars support this shelter, which faces north and is open at the back to allow light to enter.

COLLEGE IN SÃO PAULO

Marcos Acayaba

São Paulo, Brazil, 2005
Photos © Nelson Kon, Gal Oppido (archive from the FDE)

This college was built in the center of a green recreational area, within a residential setting. The dimensions of the site and its practically flat topography allowed for the construction of a very horizontal building, of only two stories. Because of its orientation, the rectangular plan of approximately 160 x 130 ft allows for a front and back courtyard, and a public area in one of the corners. This is the main entranceway for students, and also a meeting point for the occupants of the neighboring residential estate.

Three U-shaped blocks of concrete are positioned to allow space between them for a covered courtyard. Two halls, with stairs, face each other and connect these blocks.

On the ground floor, one of the blocks, with a direct entrance from the street, houses the kitchen and dining area. Opposite this are the study and reading rooms. At the entrance to the college, the largest volume is occupied, on one side by the administration building and on the other by the bathrooms and canteen. The classrooms are located on the first floor.

The entire college enjoys abundant natural light; so much so that it is filtered by an arrangement of numerous low-cost concrete sunshades. These sunshades lend strong character to the school's aesthetics.

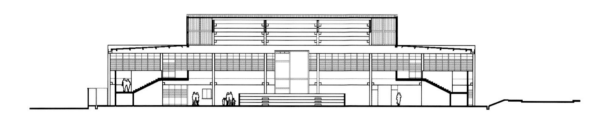

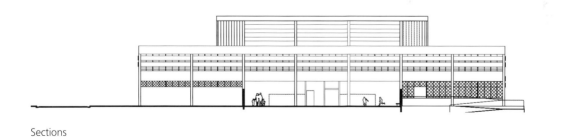

Sections

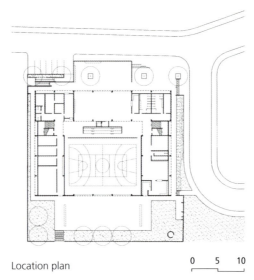

Location plan

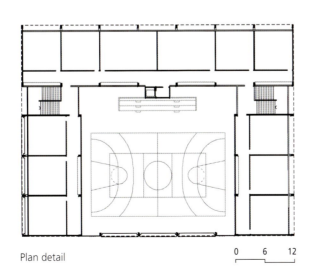

Plan detail

0 6 12

From outside, the center is composed of various cubes covered in strips of white fir wood. The nursery, music room and the building that houses the boilers are located around a large rectangle, which acts as a car park.

KINDERGARTEN IN EGG

Dietrich Untertrifaller

Egg, Austria, 2004
Photos © Bruno Klomfar

This center for children stems from a larger educational venue and is located on a clearing next to the Bregenzer Ache stream, in the Austrian city of Egg.

To ensure the safe access of the children, the entranceway to the nursery is through an atrium. The school, for two groups, occupies the entire ground floor. The classrooms, clad in light colored wood, face south. A wooden porch acts as an anteroom to the classrooms and offers a covered outdoor area, as well as protecting the windows from the effects of the sun and from bad weather. On the other side of the passageway, facing north, is a small classroom for smaller groups and a teachers' room. In order to avoid hearing the upstairs music room, this northern part of the building has been built in reinforced concrete, while on the upper floor and for the larger classrooms the structure is wooden. The floor is covered in orange polyurethane to bring more color to the rooms. The walls and ceilings are clad in birch plywood. The passageways reveal the untreated concrete.

The music room, which has a separate entrance, includes a hall that precedes this large rehearsal space. The walls, covered in plywood, and the floor of fir wood floorboards provide unbeatable acoustics.

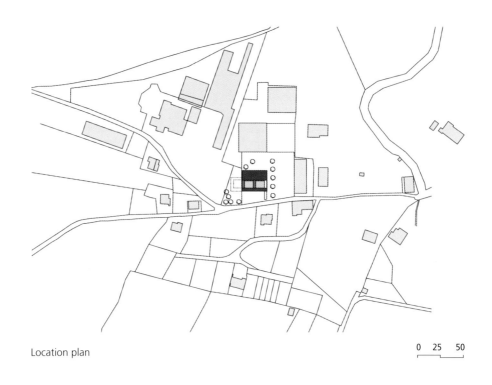

Location plan

0 25 50

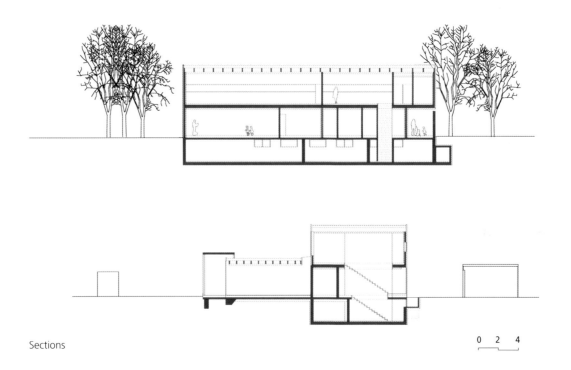

Sections

0 2 4

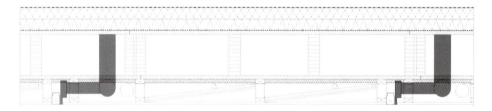

Detail of acoustic ceiling

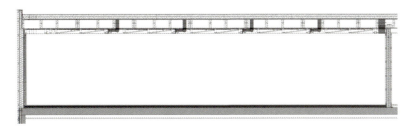

Section of acoustic ceiling

The building's roof is covered by stone from the local quarry, which is also used in the façade's pre-fabricated surfaces, as the concrete and the stone are of the same color. This same quarry has been used to reconstruct the medieval walls.

PRIMARY SCHOOL IN CROATIA

Randić Turato

City of Krk, Island Krk, Croatia, 2005
Photos © Robert Les

After much deliberation, the county council and members of the community finally agreed to locate the Fran Krsto Frankopan primary school in the north-eastern end of the medieval center of the city of Krk, on the same site as its predecessor.

The idea of replacing the previous school arose primarily from the authorities' desire to change the layout of the city, which is excessively dominated by the façade of this 19th century building. Also, the construction of the new school allowed for an archaeological excavation of the area and the part reconstruction of the city's medieval walls.

For this reason the new project had to be designed so its floor plan would respect the prominence of the wall and nearby churches. The project had to minimize the size of the school, where possible, since an excessively large complex would look out of place with the historic quarter. The barriers between the school and the city were, therefore, eliminated, so that it could integrate with the city and be divided by the city's streets. Thus, to access the sports hall students must cross a public thoroughfare. This feature transforms the school's more open buildings, such as the cafeteria, into public places. The same is the case with the path that is next to the wall and leads to the school, which is open to the public from the garden at the northern end down to the nursery. The first year classrooms have courtyards in front of them, while those of the older years back directly onto the city walls.

Location plan

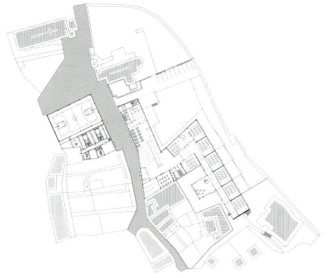

Complex plan

0 15 30

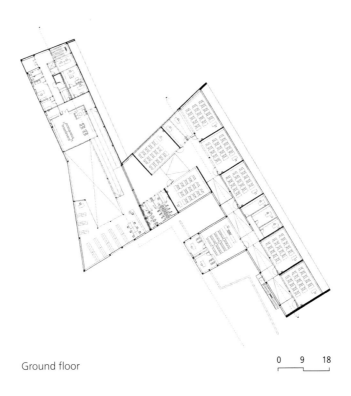

Ground floor

0 9 18

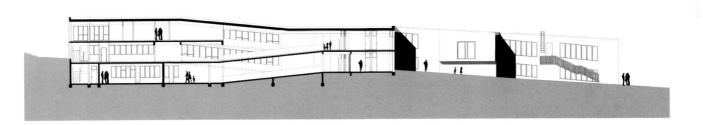

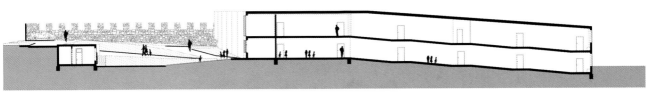

Sections

0 2 4

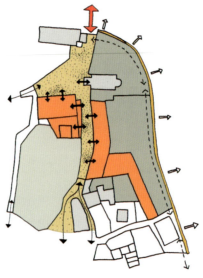
Sketch

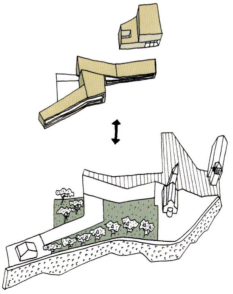

Sketch

The wood used in the structures allows a certain amount of flexibility in the finishes and saves the builders using potentially toxic materials when assembling the joins between beams and panels. This seems especially appropriate since the occupants of the building are children.

BUBBLETECURE

Shuhei Endo

Shiga, Japan, 2003
Photos © Yoshiharu Matsumura

A recently built residential area, situated 45 minutes from Osaka, is the site for this nursery with four classrooms, a games area and a hall. The building is situated in an educational complex with other educational centers, among them a primary and a secondary school. The underlying idea for the project was to offer a new architectural concept for a new generation, that of the 21st century. The dominance of wood for the surfaces responds to a criterion of respect for the environment.

The structure of the volume is based on several interconnected concrete blocks covered by shell-shaped wooden roofs. The roofs are formed from continuous triangular surfaces. This geometrically consistent design is very versatile and can be adapted to roofs of highly diverse structure types. The beams, which interweave to form the roof, measure 8 feet long and are lined by hexagonal steel panels. The geometric simplicity of this pattern favors surfaces with very varied forms.

The size of the different bubbles that the complex is split into depends on the space required by the different tasks and activities that will take place there. Logically, the two-story block and that which houses the games area need more space, which poses no problems at all given the capacity of the framework to extend infinitely.

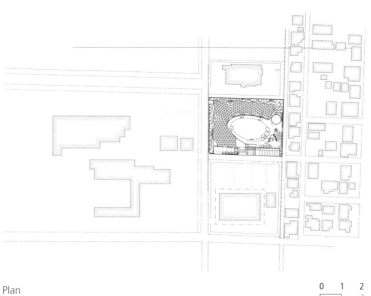

Plan

0 1 2

East elevation

West elevation

North elevation

South elevation

Sections

0 2 4

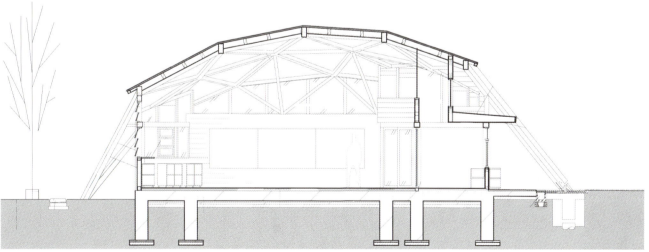
Construction detail

The project optimizes the natural light and ventilation. The materials used follow strict criteria of respect for the environment and of low toxicity, making the Clackamas institute a healthy building, deserving of awards such as the LEED Silver.

SECONDARY INSTITUTE OF CLACKAMAS

Boora Architects

Clackamas, OR, United States, 2002
Photos © Michael Mathers

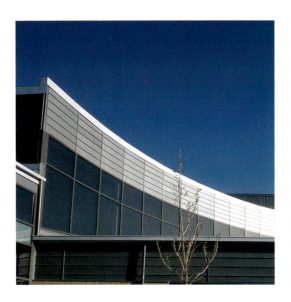

This center of secondary education for 1800 students occupies a site 8 miles to the southeast of Portland. The complex is divided into four two-story blocks that share a library. There is a large communal hall in the center for the administration areas and tutorial offices. This hallway connects the classrooms with the area for special education, the school hall and the sports facilities. From the central courtyard there is a marvelous panoramic view of the nearby Mount Hood.
The division by educational area responds to criteria of flexibility and of creating spaces for social interaction within the school community. To motivate the designers, it was stipulated that the expenses saved, thanks to the project (that would exceed the 44 % saving predicted for the first two years), would be divided in equal parts between the institute and the architects. The result of the project is an incredibly ecological complex, which takes full advantage of the light conditions, natural ventilation and possible energy savings.
The project's premises, based on environmental awareness, energy efficiency and efficient use of resources, have resulted in a dynamic center designed to favor learning and to act as support for the whole community.

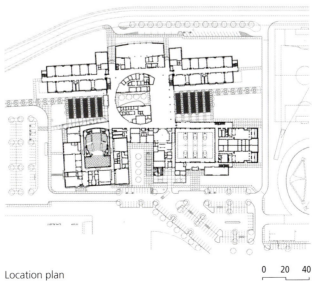

Location plan

0 20 40

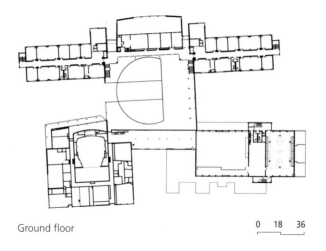

Ground floor　　　　　　　　　　　0　18　36

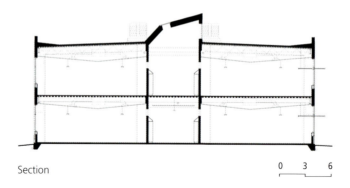

Section　　　　　　　　　　　　　0　3　6

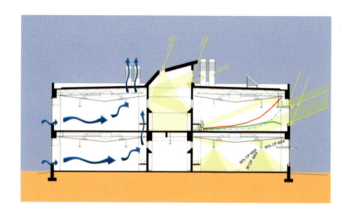

Lights and ventilations

The upper windows and the skylights in the roof significantly increase the light in the passageways.

The structure of perforated walls favors the entry of natural light, which, in turn, determines the atmosphere of each space. Likewise, the different colors used mark an itinerary of activities and underline the contrast between the open and closed spaces.

KINDERGARTEN IN PEDEROBBA

C+S Associati

Pederobba, Italy, 2005
Photos © Alessandra Chemollo, Carlo Cappai

Surrounded by vineyards and wheat fields and located next to the small historic quarter, this nursery has been inserted into the simple urban landscape of Covolo. The newly built buildings face southeast and rise to the height of a single story, so as not to look out of place with the surrounding constructions. Their horizontal profile merges with the plains of crops that surround them. The form that these volumes evoke is as simple as that of a wall, sometimes doubled, which faces south, as do the traditional barns in the area.

The south façade has three large doors protected by canopies, which filter the entry of natural light. A succession of glass sliding doors links the classrooms with the outside and helps to integrate the garden with the educational complex.

The north façade is more compact and delineates the access to the service area, which includes the laundry room, the boiler and the kitchens. A longitudinal axis running from east to west acts as a backbone to the classrooms. This street is signed with different colors indicating the different ways to the entrances, the classrooms, the common areas, or the teachers' room. The street ends in a large central space that joins all the project's elements; the open entrance to the garden, the cafeteria and the classrooms.

Plan

0 3 6

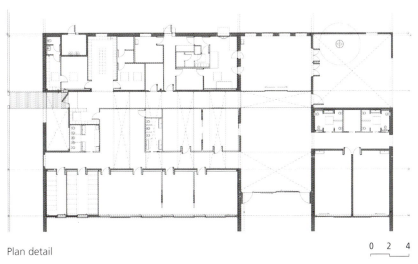
Plan detail

Sections

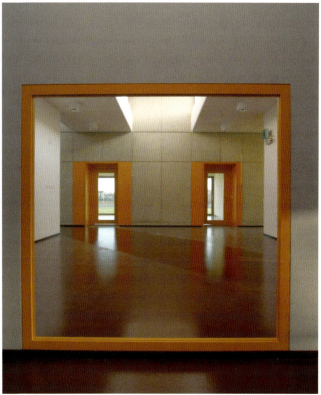

Construction detail

The brick façades are covered, in parts, with wooden panels. Although brown and red shades have been used, which link it with the surrounding buildings, the predominant blue brick is the distinguishing mark that allows this building to be recognized as the community's neurological center.

WESTERN HOUSE PRIMARY SCHOOL

ADP Architects

Cippenham, United Kingdom, 2006
Photos © Jonathan Moore

The recent urban development of Cippenham alerted the Slough Borough council to the need to create a new primary school in the suburbs with a capacity for some 400 pupils. The architects proposed a building that would stand out as a landmark in the neighborhood but without disregarding criteria of profitability and functionality. The new construction, which uses sustainable materials, pays particular attention to the area of natural ventilation and is divided into two blocks, connected via the entrance atrium. One of these blocks, which is two stories high, houses the hall, the library, communal areas and the classrooms for the older students. In the other building, just a single-story, are the classrooms for the younger pupils, the nursery and the teachers' areas.

All the classrooms face south, back on to the games areas and have views of Windsor Castle. The communal areas and the teachers' area occupy the northern side, and are somewhat separated to offer greater privacy, and to allow for their use by the community without having to open the entire school.

The complex has two roads, for entry and exit, which connect it with the nearby motorway. The buildings act as a barrier between the noise of the traffic from the motorway and the games area and sports tracks.

Plan

0 2 4

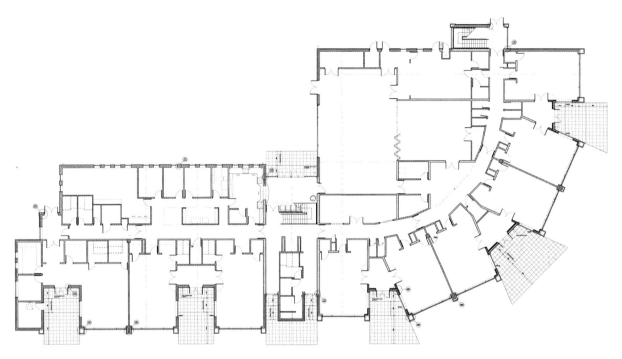
Ground floor

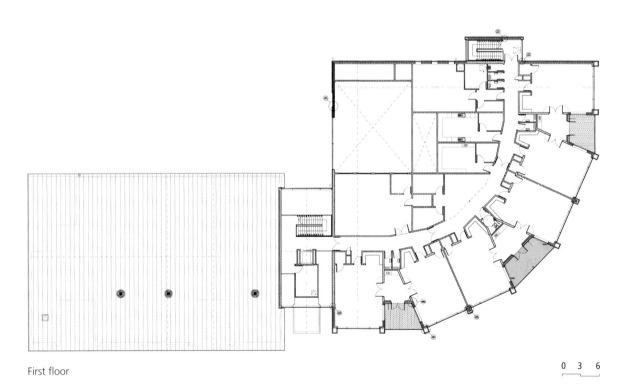
First floor

0 3 6

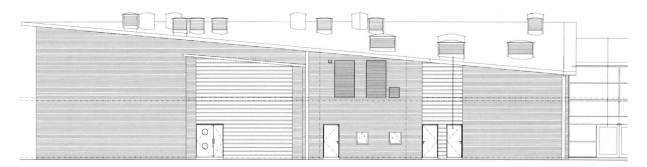

North elevation

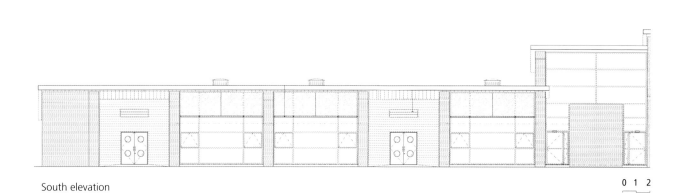

South elevation

0 1 2

The school is located on top of a hill in the center of the village, and has been designed as both a school and a meeting and cultural space for the local people.

MINAMI YAMASHIRO PRIMARY SCHOOL

Richard Rogers Partnership

Kyoto, Japan, 2003
Photos © Katsuhisa Kida

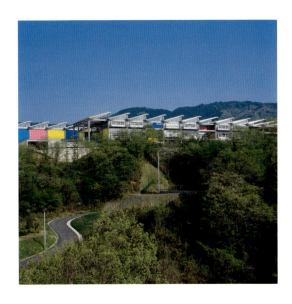

The mountainous southern area of Kyoto is the setting for this primary school, designed partly to combat the fall in the area's population. The idea was for this community and schooling center to become a symbol of identity for the village and unite the community.

The 66,700 ft^2 college has been designed as a large house, where not only school activities take place, but also in the evenings classes are given for the adult population.

The project makes use of the simplest of materials and features, producing elegant results, which are easily maintained. Flexibility is the fundamental concept behind the design, to the extent that the layouts mean classrooms can change between time periods, i.e. morning and afternoon, and the spaces can be adequate for the different curricular needs of the future. The contemporary structure, is markedly reminiscent of traditional Japanese architecture. Outside, the spaces of wall between the grid frame are painted in different colors depending on the area their functions correspond to.

A large communal hall is located between the two floors of flexible spaces that house the classrooms and outdoor playing fields. On the lower floor there are specific areas for art, science and music rooms. The sloping panels on the roof leave space for large skylights, which flood the interior of the building with natural light.

Elevation

0 15 30

Ground floor

0 15 30

First floor

0 15 30

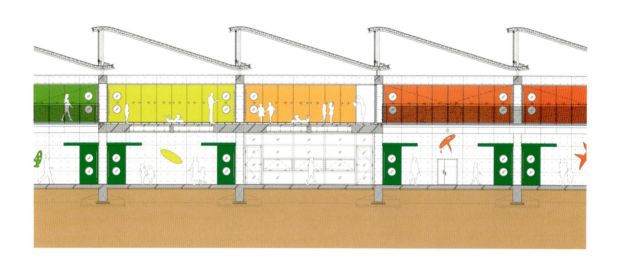
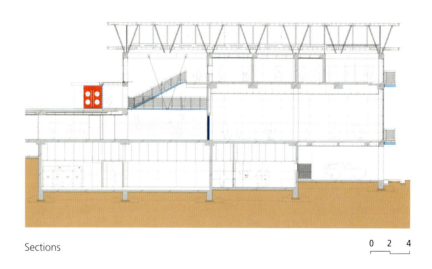

Sections   0 2 4

The skylights that light the interior of the new building are shaped like chimneys with igloos on top. Their presence in the upper square constitutes a small sculptural display.

KINDERGARTEN IN LEISACH

Machnè Architekten

Lienz, Austria, 2004
Photos © Paul Ott

This project, carried out by the Machnè studio, consisted in adding a building to house the kindergarten of a pre-existing primary school. Also, the original volume had to be given new windows and a modern heat insulation system. One of the requisites for the extension was to leave the garden to the west of the site in tact, to remain as a green area.

It was important that the new volume respected the topography of the original structure, so building practically the entire space beneath ground level minimized its visual impact. This way the extension to this educational center could be carried out without any negative consequences for the original structures. At the level of the school entrance, a large play area has been created for the pupils.

The concrete roof slopes lightly upwards at the south end, to facilitate an adequate flow of natural light into the interior of the subterranean volume. The surface is occupied by a small square that serves as a meeting point.

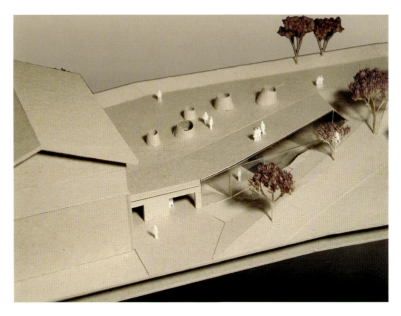

Scale model

Basement   0 5 10

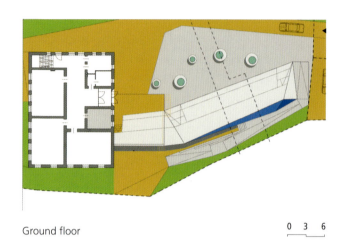

Ground floor   0 3 6

South elevation   0 4 8

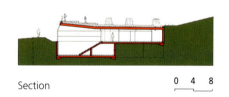

Section   0 4 8

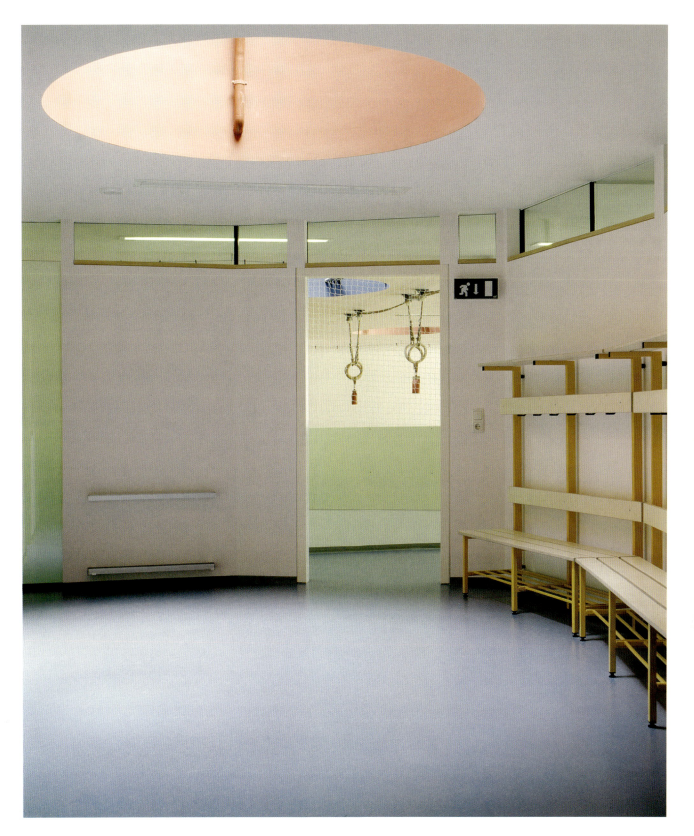

The extensions to the building consist of structures clad in metal plates with roofs arranged in lightly sloping planes. These planes extend from adjacent spaces leaving openings for the windows.

PRIMARY SCHOOL IN BABYLON

Gruzen Samton Architects

New York, NY, United States, 2003
Photos © John Woodruff, Peter Brown

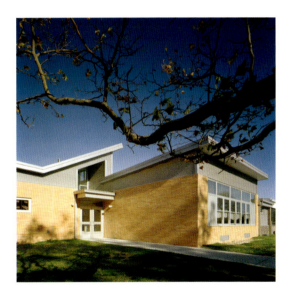

This complex project taken on by Gruzen Samton Architects consisted, among other constructions, in extending the constructed surface area by more than 3200 ft². In fact, in the end the original extension of the space was doubled. Also, an exhaustive renovation of the interior had to be carried out to adapt the center to a series of changes to the curriculum and educational program. Two wings were therefore added to the pre-existing building, and the old cafeteria was renovated along with one of the classrooms of the nursery. A new entrance and collection point for cars has also been added.

The new wing, that includes the bookshop and sports hall, connects with the main entrance hallway through a new communal area. The opposite wing has nine new classrooms, with spaces especially designed for music and art rooms. Each of the new rooms has been designed following criteria that emphasize the separation between the reading areas and other communal areas, such as the library, and computer room, given the social function that the center has after school hours. The new spaces comply with the aim of motivating study and learning, as well as the exchange of ideas, for which special attention was paid to making communal areas, such as the corridors, more comfortable. The new classroom block has been located next to the courtyard to take advantage of the natural light, and with the idea that the latter may, in the future, host a gardened space and an outdoor classroom.

Location plan

0 15 30

Ground floor

0 15 30

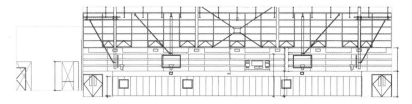

East elevation

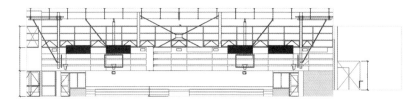

West elevation

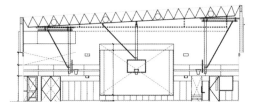

North elevation

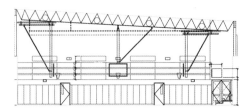

South elevation

0 2 4

The classrooms are large, luminous spaces, which adapt to a multitude of activities that take place in the school. The dynamic combination of colors and shapes of the buildings' exterior continues here.

EXPANSION OF ARAGON AVENUE ELEMENTARY SCHOOL

John Friedman-Alice Kimm Architects

Los Angeles, CA, United States, 2006
Photos © Benny Chan/Fotoworks

The extension of this primary school, situated in the Cypress Park neighborhood, forms part of an ambitious, low-budget program carried out by the "Los Angeles Unified School District". The project is composed of three new volumes. The largest of these is a three-story building with a total surface area of 32,800 square feet, occupied by a car park and sixteen classrooms, two of which are kindergartens. A large door and stairs marks the entrance to this building. A 1500 square foot pavilion housing the kitchen and an outdoor dining area of 3000 square feet constitute the other two constructions, completing the project. The joining of the two classroom buildings forms a U shape and delineates the central courtyard. Uncovered bleachers and concrete stairs descend from the main entrance down to a large courtyard, situated on a lower level. However, it is the color and designs on the façades that have generated a new identity for the school. The limited budget lead architects to use this resource, which has succeeded in making the new structures more dynamic. The pattern on the plastered façades draws on the colorful houses close to the school. Also, an orthogonal shape has been used in the structures to turn the buildings into an inspirational feature for the students.

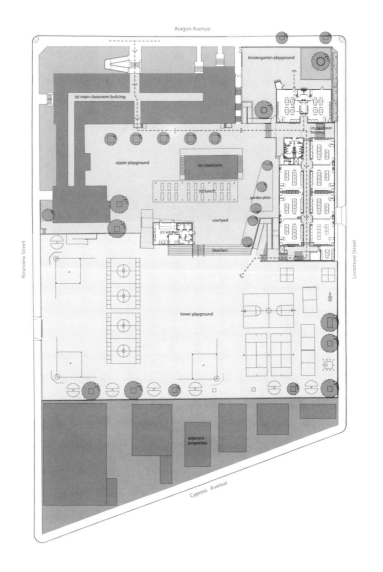

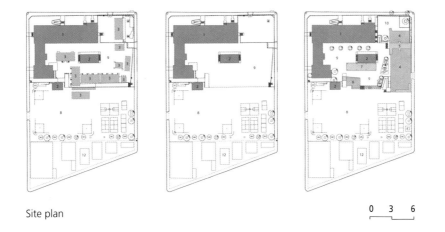

Site plan

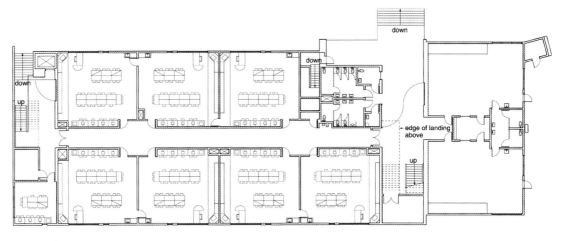

Existing plan

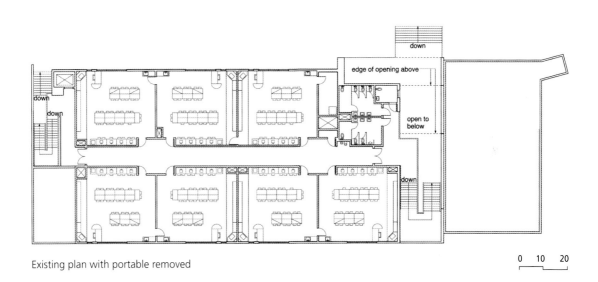

Existing plan with portable removed

0   10   20

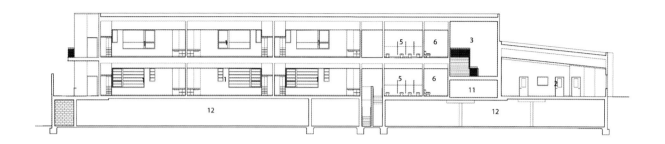

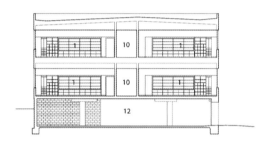

Proposed plans

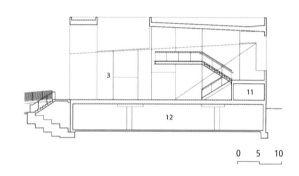

0 5 10

North elevation

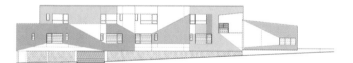

East elevation

South elevation

West elevation

0 10 20

The classrooms are large, luminous spaces, which adapt to a multitude of activities that take place in the school. The dynamic combination of colors and shapes of the buildings' exterior continues here.

The facilities in the sports center allow for the practice of a wide range of sports.
Covered running tracks and a climbing wall can be seen here in the photo.

BUNDESGYMNASIUM BLUDENZ

Hermann Kaufmann

Bludenz, Austria, 2005
Photos © Bruno Klomfar

A respect for the existing architecture and good use of the natural light are two of the most striking features of this renovation. The use of color in circulation areas and of poems written on the walls transforms this area into a unique and special place.

The renovation of this school, formed by a school building and a sports center, has been carried out with maximum respect to the original construction, which holds architectural importance. The school was built in 1956 and the sports area in 1975. The renovation has lasted three years, during which time 930 students and 90 teachers have shown great patience. The architect Hermann Kaufmann respected the constructive lines and carried out the renovation in accordance with them. In the western area, where the dining area was previously located, special classrooms have been installed for theoretical and practical classes. This new zone marks a clear difference with respect to the exterior of the school, and delineates the entire west wing. Although the dining room has been moved to the pavilion in the north wing, the internal organization and the functionality of the school has been maintained. The new educational area is supported by a reinforced concrete structure with walls of wood and glass. The glass façade allows the interior to take full advantage of the natural light. One of the most remarkable features of this renovation is the use of color in the passageways and stairs, proposed by Erich Wiesner, which has given this school an unmistakable identity. The walls of the circulation zones in this section have been completed with poems by Ernst Jandl.

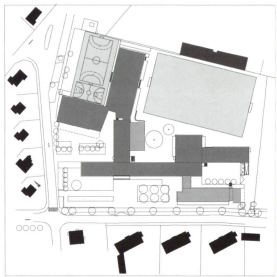

Location plan

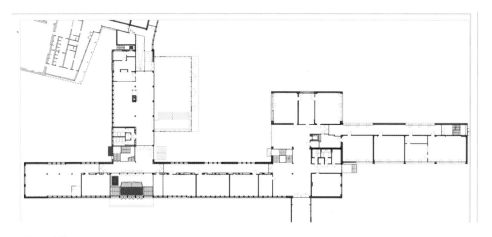

Ground floor

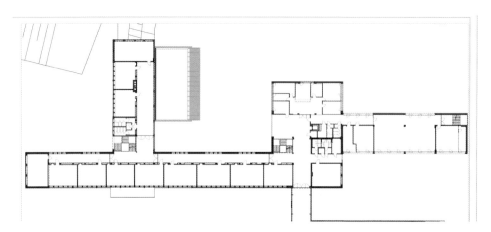

First floor

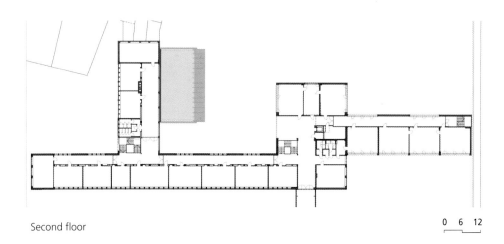

Second floor

0 6 12

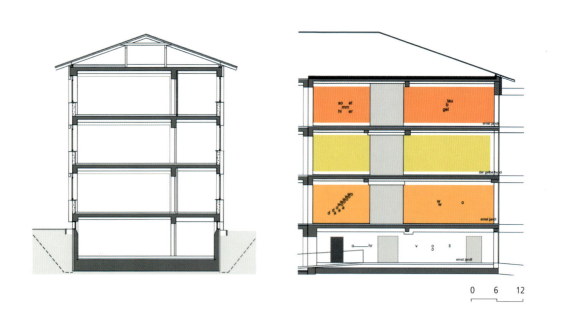
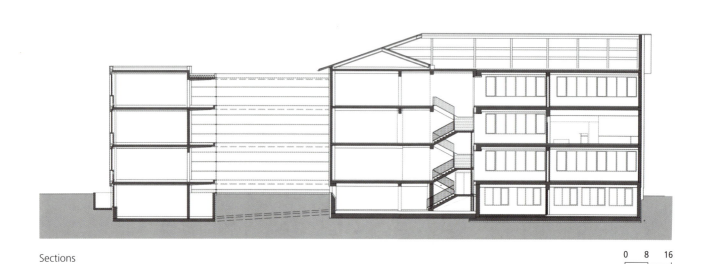

Sections

The facilities in the sports center allow for the practice of a wide range of sports. Covered running tracks and a climbing wall can be seen here in the photo.